"In this rich and poetic book, Andrea B[...]
that we can almost feel the dirt on our [...]
battle against weeds and bugs, the joy o[...]
But far more than that, she plants in us as readers a desire for [...]
richly in us, ridding us of what will choke out spiritual life and beauty, and
growing in us abundant fruit of his Spirit."

> NANCY GUTHRIE, bible teacher and author of numerous books,
> including *Even Better than Eden: Nine Ways the Bible's Story
> Changes Everything about Your Story*

"Andrea's poetic reflections on the gospel through the lens of gardening are
simply stunning. Her writing invites readers into a slower, more observant,
and appreciative way of thinking. Those who love to garden will relate, those
who've never planted will want to start, and all will want to open the Word
and rest in the Master Gardner himself."

> EMILY A. JENSEN, author of *He Is Strong:
> Devotions For When You Feel Weak*

*"A Bit of Earth* is a bit of godly wisdom to add to our understanding of
creation and our relationship with our Creator. In a time when humanity
has abandoned God's natural provision in favor of synthetic substitutes and
harmful concoctions called 'food,' Christians are rightly cautioned to return
to his garden for sustenance. Filling one's larder (and belly) with the miraculous
bounty that God has gifted us improves human health, self-reliance, food
security, and nurtures the soil. It also imbues in us the humility and gratitude
that have been abandoned by a society that has turned away from God. The
whole world groans for all of God. He can be seen clearly in *A Bit of Earth*."

> JOHN KLAR, pastor, attorney, and author of *Small Farm Republic:
> Why Conservatives Must Embrace Local Agriculture, Reject Climate
> Alarmism, and Lead an Environmental Revival*

"There's far more of heaven in the dirt than you might realize. In *A Bit of
Earth*, theologian/gardener Andrea Burke closes the gap between the sacred
and the mundane, and points out the deep connections between seasons on
earth and seasons in heaven."

> KEVIN MALONEY, lead pastor, Grace Road Church,
> Rochester, New York

"If a Christian poet kept a garden journal it might read like Andrea Burke's *A Bit of Earth*. This book is beautifully written, richly observant, deeply felt, and—perhaps best of all—practical. Those who want to tend their own 'bit of earth' and those looking for a devotional with depth would do well to seek out this treasure."

CHRISTIE PURIFOY, author of *Garden Maker*
and *Seedtime and Harvest*

"There are recipes in this book: plans carefully plotted out on graph paper for how to grow toward resurrection day. Touch earth with Andrea Burke."

E. M. WELCHER, pastor, Grace Baptist Church,
Vermillion, South Dakota

"Burke does something completely unique in this collection of stunning essays, offering her readers the chance to dig their hands deep into the earth of both their gardens and their spiritual lives."

RACHEL WELCHER, poet and author
of *Sometimes Women Lie About Being Okay*

"Andrea Burke has a unique ability to find depth and beauty in the simple things of life and then find the perfect words to help others see them as well. *A Bit of Earth* offers the perfect blend of poetic and practical writing as the reader is encouraged to see the goodness of the Lord in and through his creation. You do not have to be a gardener or farmer to be blessed by this book."

CODY WILBANKS, teaching pastor, Grace Road Church,
Rochester, New York

"As she reflects on her own careful cultivation of her garden, Andrea Burke's tender and devotionally rich writing in *A Bit of Earth* will cultivate vital growth in your own heart. This is a beautiful book."

JARED C. WILSON, assistant professor of pastoral ministry
and author in residence at Midwestern Baptist Theological Seminary;
staff pastor for preaching and director of the pastoral training center
at Liberty Baptist Church, Kansas City, Missouri

# A BIT OF
# EARTH

## A YEAR IN THE GARDEN WITH GOD

# A BIT OF
# EARTH

## A YEAR IN THE GARDEN WITH GOD

Andrea G. Burke

LEXHAM PRESS

*A Bit of Earth: A Year in the Garden with God*

Copyright 2024 Andrea G. Burke

Lexham Press, 1313 Commercial St., Bellingham, WA 98225
LexhamPress.com

You may use brief quotations from this resource in presentations, articles, and books. For all other uses, please write Lexham Press for permission. Email us at permissions@lexhampress.com.

Unless otherwise noted, Scripture quotations are from the *ESV® Bible* *(The Holy Bible, English Standard Version®)*, copyright © 2001 by Crossway Bibles, a publishing ministry of Good News Publishers. Used by permission. All rights reserved.

The seasonal artwork at the beginning of each section is original to the author.

Print ISBN 9781683597421
Digital ISBN 9781683597438
Library of Congress Control Number 2023949562

Lexham Editorial: Todd Hains, Mandi Newell, Jessi Strong
Cover Design: Jonathan Myers
Typesetting: Abigail Stocker

24 25 26 27 28 29 / US / 12 11 10 9 8 7 6 5 4 3 2

*For Madeleine and Callan—*
*of all the growing things in this untamed world,*
*you two are my favorite.*


*For Jed—*
*there is no square inch of dirt on this earth*
*that I want more than the bit we're standing on.*

# Contents

Acknowledgments *xi*

## WINTER

1. The Final Death  *3*
2. The Work of the Cold  *9*
3. The Days of Rest  *14*
4. Counting the Seeds  *17*
5. The Waiting Season  *22*
6. Hidden Friends  *27*
7. The Winter Table  *31*
8. Hidden in Winter  *40*
9. The Empty Season  *44*
10. Grief  *49*
11. The Days of Dark  *54*
12. The Lonely Season  *59*
13. The Dark and Tender Season  *63*

## SPRING

14. The Late Snow  *71*
15. Stuck: The Mud Season  *75*
16. The Prep Season  *80*
17. Watch the Birds  *86*
18. Planting and Tending Seeds and the Starts  *90*
19. Potting Up, Hardening Off, and Withstanding Winds  *95*
20. The Return of Life  *103*
21. The Thinning Season  *106*
22. The Resurrection Season  *111*
23. The Stormy Season  *113*
24. The War of the Weeds, *Part One*  *118*

## SUMMER

25　The War of the Weeds, *Part Two*　*127*
26　The All-Consuming Season　*132*
27　Good Fences Make Good Neighbors　*137*
28　The Pruning Season　*142*
29　The Hidden Fruit　*147*
30　The Mimic Weeds　*151*
31　The Storms of Destruction　*156*
32　After the Storm　*162*
33　The Garden Pests　*167*
34　The Heat　*173*
35　Blood, Sweat, and Tears: The War of the Summer Garden　*178*
36　Easy Fruit and Abundant Harvests　*182*
37　The Days of Light　*186*

## AUTUMN

38　The Lord of the Harvest　*193*
39　The Fall Garden　*197*
40　The Feasting Season　*202*
41　Remembering Failures　*206*
42　Watch the Farmer　*210*
43　Good Soil　*214*
44　Preparing for Death　*220*
45　Preserving for Later　*226*
46　Tired and Weary Season　*233*
47　Gathering Seeds and Planting for Spring　*237*
48　Perennial Care for Next Year　*242*
49　Goodnight Garden　*247*

Chapter Epigraph Sources　*253*
Notes　*257*

# Acknowledgments

*I've learned through* this process that writing a book, while it's mostly a solitary process, relies heavily on community, friends, and texts that say "Keep going!" These are those people.

First and foremost, this book would not be in anyone's hands without the hard work and faith of my editor Rachel Joy Welcher. When I first met Rachel, I knew immediately that she was smarter and more well-spoken than I ever would be. She's formidable and wise, full of kindness and has a royal sort of excellence about her. To work with her felt like a true honor. She saw this book before it ever made it to paper and she helped breathe life into this work. She believed in it, helped shape it, read all of my *very* rough drafts, and helped give it flight. This is the book I would have only dreamed of writing and because of her, here it is.

Todd Hains, and the rest of the team at Lexham—I have found kindred hearts in Christ, and beauty across the miles and mountains. Thank you for believing in this book and a relatively no-name writer from New York.

Kevin Maloney, Cody Wilbanks, Abbey Sitterley, Nicole Dumas, Kasey Moffett, and the rest of the staff and family at

Grace Road Church, for hearing my regular updates and fears and insecurities about this little book. And for relentlessly cheering me on.

Ashley and Ryan Kirnan are in these pages more than they realize. No two people in our lives understand our love for the land and growing things as much as they do. Ashley, when this is done, let's order more seeds. Also I promised Brynlee I'd get her name in here somewhere. Check.

My entire family of in-laws who put up with me working on this book for several of the last family gatherings. I spent a few long weekends with my laptop open in front of me, trying to pin down words that tumbled over in my mind. I promise I wasn't trying to avoid you. I know I won the in-law lottery and I only hope you're all okay with getting this book for Christmas, or your birthday, or whatever the next gift exchange is.

My sister, Dee, who first showed me Tasha Tudor, Gladys Taber, Susan Branch, Thoreau, Frederic Edwin Church, Olana, and the like. For years and years, unbeknownst to you (and me!), you laid the groundwork for all of this. Where would I be without them, without you?

My mom and dad have proudly put up with my writings since I first learned how to string letters together. My poetry verses at five were pretty "special," apparently, because they held onto them all of these years later. Mom and Dad, thank you for being my first audience, my first reviewers, my first applause at library

## Acknowledgments

readings, and for giving me the foundation to think I could maybe write a book someday. My father always told me, "Find out what you love to do and figure out a way to get paid for it." Well Dad, I did it. Also, the reason I have most of the perennials I have is because my father makes sure my mailbox is filled with new deliveries every spring and fall. I would have zero tulips if it weren't for him. Mom, you've never left my side—a forever friend in every wave of writing, dreaming, and starting over again. Your poetry was written on my life. Thank you.

Mr. Clayton, my high school English teacher—he called this when I was just 17. In AP English, he planted something in the heart of this country girl in a tiny high school in the middle of nowhere, and I've never forgotten it. I hope this makes you proud.

The old farmer and his wife from Macroom—"in my memory I will always see the town I loved so well."

To every farmer I've ever met and never met—you keep food on our tables and understand far more about any of this than I ever will.

Madeleine, my daughter—aren't you glad we went to McDonalds together that one night? You got to be there for the call that this book was going to happen and I'm so thrilled we got to share that moment. And for all those late night encouraging hugs and laughs in the kitchen when I was delirious, for watching *The Office* while I tried to find the right words, and for being my friend in the garden when I'm excited about cucamelons and potatoes—thank you. I love you birdie.

Callan, my son—you are the best helper in the garden and I can only hope you're learning things that outlive the gardens and even me. You have the strength of your father and there's no one else I want in the garden with me when it's time to pull carrots, even if you do eat half of them. I love you Captain. Also, please, please, please stop chasing the ducks.

Jed, my husband. For every garden dream I've had, you have been next to me asking where to start digging. This book is no different. I have never doubted your belief in this little book and my ability to write it. To all the late nights, tears (mine), doubts, and fears, you've met me with strength, peace, and a reminder to persist. The anchor to all of my kite dreams—thanks for holding me steady on this one. There aren't enough words in the world, in all of the languages, to write about how much I love you but I'll spend the rest of my life trying.

The Lord gave me words, the Lord gave me a garden, the Lord keeps giving me his grace. None of this, including me, would be here without Christ's sustenance in every minute, hour, day. To God be the glory.

And finally, this book only exists because of the people in my life who kept telling me to write and who also didn't think I was a fool for planting things like ... 1,000 heads of garlic. (Or at least who didn't tell me to my face.) To all my family, friends, homeschooling girls, church members, librarians, local farmers and gardeners—this

*Acknowledgments*

book was a joy to write and I hope it's a joy to read. May your gardens grow, your weeds never go to seed, and your faith be refreshed.

# WINTER

# 1

# The Final Death

*Lord of all to thee we raise*
*This our hymn of grateful praise*

*Autumn takes its time* marching to the grave, but eventually it gets there. All while we're parading and applauding, snapping photos in corn fields and pumpkin patches, and while we rake the leaves to jump, autumn is humming a quiet dirge to the end.

The end of the season.

The end of the harvest.

The end of the color and the warmth.

The end of the light. The fading of green.

Here, the newly opened bud will not last. Here, the last rose that bloomed will turn black.

Here, the realization of all we did, all we worked for, all we planned—ends.

*Winter*

I suppose I knew it all along. The geese fly south and the grass fades, and I'm reminded that the things of this earth do not last. Will not last. Creation is established and moves in a certain cadence of hope mixed with longing, repeating itself over and over again.

And death repeats iteself over and over and over again. As though creation grieves its own loss year after year. Another year of creation groaning, waiting for redemption. Another year of humanity exhausting the land we were made to steward. Another year of tired dirt giving up more for us to consume, ready now for a long winter's nap.

All summer long the trees of the field clapped their hands, and now the leaves fade into a copper song of praise before they fall to the ground. The garden gives us one final burst of vegetation and flora. One final bouquet, filled mostly with strawflower and zinnia. The last jalapeno harvest. With one last dig for carrots into the cold soil, and with a handful of winter greens and dirt-covered root vegetables, I take a quiet walk through before we say "goodnight" and close the gate. The cold has come on faster than I anticipated, and I'm not wearing a coat heavy enough to guard me from the way it wants to crawl inside my bones. My son, Callan, decides he's had enough and runs to the porch door, calling for me to follow him into the warm glow of our house. The gate lock slides like ice under my fingertips. It's a gentle kindness to know this death is coming, but it still pulls heavy on my heart. It drags at my feet through the decay. I know we must walk here. I know it's necessary and just as beautiful and sacred as every other day of wonder I've walked through.

Today's wonder, however, is locked on the sky—the sun has moved farther south, the clouds swirl like snow, the moon's glow feels colder than I remember. The garden glistens under the frost, a kiss of death to all that remained. It's over now.

Death always cuts with a cold knife. It stills the blood in the roots, in the leaves, in our own hearts as it steals away life. Even though we know resurrection will come, we're still faced with the emptiness that winter carves out of us, leaving us more hollow than we were before. More hollow, sometimes, than we even realized we could be. Even when you see it coming, even when the winds whip around the beds, the final exhale is just that—final.

A dear friend of mine died somewhat unexpectedly last winter. She had fallen ill and was hospitalized for further care. Because of local Covid restrictions, I wasn't able to see her. I got hospital updates from her family members. I texted her, but her energy was low and her responses were brief. Few details. One afternoon, in the middle of a typical homeschool day, my phone lit up with her name. I answered only to hear her raspy breath.

"Andrea?" she said in between short breaths. "Please," she took a breath, " ... pray." And so I did, without hesitation. I prayed and listened to her labored sounds. She couldn't even form a full sentence. I prayed a prayer that I cannot even remember. It was short and before I hung up, she managed to repeat, "I love you. I love you. I love you."

A few days later she called again, a bit easier this time. She told me she was tired. She wanted to go home. She wanted to be back in her house. She wanted out of the hospital. "But even if he doesn't bring me home, we know he's sovereign. We'll be together again someday," she reminded me.

She went home to be with Jesus just a few days later.

Even though I could see it coming—the leaves, the sky, the moon, her breathing, her voice—it still did not take away the sharp edge of the end.

*I love you. I love you. I love you.* I feel this at the end of all things. The end of the garden. The end of autumn. The end of life. Here we can still see how love persists in-between labored breaths.

*I love you. I love you. I love you.* This repeated song from creation to its Creator, even as it bends low to submit to the way of the earth.

*I love you. I love you. I love you.* The song I know my Savior sings to all his people, even as we face grief, the decay, and the end.

> All flesh is grass,
> > and all its beauty is like the flower of the field.
> The grass withers, the flower fades
> > when the breath of the LORD blows on it;
> > surely the people are grass.
> The grass withers, the flower fades,
> > but the word of our God will stand forever.
>
> (Isaiah 40:6b–8)

## Cultivate

English poet George Herbert writes about death in his poem "Time":

> For where thou onely wert before
> An executioner at best;
> Thou art a gard'ner now, and more.

Pray this:

Inhale: *The grass withers*
Exhale: *Your word is forever*

Lord, I know that all flesh is like grass.
All our beauty will wither and fade.
Just like your creation, I too must look to you when death draws near.
Help me to abide in Your word while I still have breath.
Quicken my cold heart by your Spirit to pray.
Teach me to number my days
so I might gain a heart of wisdom.
Show me how to love like you loved,
even in my fading moments, even in the brevity of life.
You who loved, even as you died on the cross.
You, the Word, remained.
Help me to see you as Paul does in Colossians 1:

*Winter*

  The image of the invisible God,
  the firstborn over all creation.
  In you all things were created:
  things in heaven and on earth,
  visible and invisible,
    whether thrones or powers or rulers or authorities;
    all things have been created through you and for you.
    You are before all things, and in you all things hold together.

Even me. You love me, you love me, you love me.

## 2

# The Work of the Cold

*Withhold not thy mercies in the night season;*
*thy hand never wearies,*
*thy power needs no repose,*
*thine eye never sleeps.*

*As hints of winter* begin to arrive on the horizon in late autumn, it's time to get your garlic, shallots, and any other bulbs you have ready to go into the ground. A few years ago, we decided to forego the garlic harvest and saved it all for seed. Baskets of beautiful garlic sat waiting for months on end until we put the entire crop back into the ground. But that year of "going without" (and by without, I mean we went to the grocery store and bought it there!) meant that we had enough to harvest the following year to last us through the next season, as well as enough to plant for seed again. In the span of one year, we became self-sufficient in garlic. I could now offer kale and garlic to our "end of the world" plan, which does not appeal to my family. Garlic as a means of survival is certainly a hard sell.

In that stretch of pre-holiday time during late October and November, before the holidays completely take over life, it's time for us to plant the garlic and shallots, one by one, in the ground. It feels like such an act of faith. To plant something in the northeast, right on the cusp of winter, feels almost foolish. How will it survive winter? I barely do. I feel a kinship with these small cloves that get pushed into the earth. Winter tucks me in; buries me. Some days winter feels safe; other days, suffocating. Yet, as the one who does the work of tending the winter planting, I've learned that the cold isn't the end—just the way through. I have seen, year after year, how the work of one chilly November afternoon pays off in July. Clove by clove, I press them into the dark earth. Even the soil is preparing for winter. I can tell with each push, my fingers getting a little colder and nearly cut by the hardening ground. Woolly bears, the small little predictors of winters, curl up in fuzzy balls, burying themselves just beneath the surface. The beds are covered with straw or piles of leaves we've raked up from the yard. This is their winter blanket, a thick covering of protection for those particularly harsh days and nights.

*The Farmer's Almanac* says this about garlic:

> Garlic does best if it can experience a "dormancy" period of colder weather—at least 40°F (4°C)—that lasts 4 to 8 weeks. By planting garlic bulbs in the fall, they have time to develop healthy roots before temperatures drop and/or

the ground freezes, but not enough time for the garlic to form top growth. Then, by early spring, the bulbs "wake up" from their dormancy and start rapidly producing foliage, followed by bulbs, before the harshest heat of summer stops their growth.

It's truths like this that stop me in my tracks. If everything in creation is designed to reveal the nature of God, then certainly, even garlic has something to teach me.

When I feel myself going dormant, surrounded by blankets and howling winds, and the season of fruitfulness and productivity seems to come to a screeching halt, I remember this—maybe it's time to grow roots instead of fruit. Roots that send their long hands down into the deeper depths, the more hidden places, the quieter, sleeping hollows where water, nutrients, and stability can be anchored. There where the Spirit of God already knows how to bring life, hovering over the depths and waters and darkness. A place to sleep and recover, a place to rest; a place to wait.

We often view the cold as some kind of punishment or withdrawal of beauty. I suppose living in the north has taught me that the cold invites a certain kind of beauty that not many other seasons provide. This is when we draw near, we light candles, the dinner steams and tea steeps, and all of my old quilts, especially the ones made by my mother, are stacked against the wall for every person who would want one. As Gladys Taber said, "All our blankets have stories about them." Comfort, coziness, hygge, whatever you'd like to call it—it does something for us. It's why the simple image of a small house with warm, lit windows in the middle of a winter countryside is so inviting. We know there's a place we belong in the cold and it's not to simply endure, but to step in, step closer, slow down, grab a blanket, tell a story, fall asleep.

All winter long, I wonder how those small cloves are doing. Buried under snow, it's impossible to know. But faithfully, every spring, they wake up. Their small green heads break through the mulch cover to say good morning to a yawning world. It works only because they grew roots and rested. If only we could learn these same rhythms. Root, rest, grow. To the young mother who hasn't slept, the tired pastor faithfully preaching each Sunday, the struggling husband or wife who has lost hope in their marriage, the college student who feels overwhelmed, the doubter, the weary, the wrestling one—resist the urge to present a perfect outward image and instead, go deep. Grow roots and rest. Cease your striving to produce something that it simply is not time for. The cold is not the end; it's just the way through. Dormancy is not the same as death. It's OK to breathe. Light a candle and hold on.

## Cultivate

If you plan to plant garlic, shallots, or seeds for some perennials (in my zone, the fall is when we plant foxglove, larkspur, and poppies), now is the time to do those things! A good rule of thumb for planting garlic is to make sure they have enough time to get some roots before the cold hits and they go dormant, but not too much time. You don't want them breaking through the surface before winter hits, so don't plant too early. If you're in a colder zone with harsh weather, nestle them in with straw for the long winter nap. As you prepare yourself for the cold, look for the places you might need to step back and rest. Entrust the Lord with these things.

Father, help us to remember that the cold you send
 is meant to refresh us.
As the teacher reminds us in Proverbs 25:13,

> Like the cold of snow in the time of harvest
> is a faithful messenger to those who send him;
> he refreshes the soul of his masters.

Refresh our souls with your message, O Lord.
Let the snow wash away the sweat and dirt of our striving.
Help us to follow you into the cold,
knowing you have already placed in us the things we'll need on the other side.

# 3

# The Days of Rest

*I am glad you are here with me.*
*Here at the end of all things, Sam.*

*Lord, I have closed* the greenhouse door. I have hung up the aprons and my gloves, the trowels, the spades, the baskets. There are no more seeds to collect. I have harvested the last of what I could find. I have preserved the remaining fruit. All of the herbs, potatoes, squash, pods, any remnants of the garden, have now found their winter homes and I am done.

I am tired. My cuticles are dry and raw. My work clothes are threadbare and my shoes have seen better days. I have seen every season of growth and suffering, work and toil, sweat and blood, loss and joy, and here I find myself at the end of one season but not nearly at the beginning of the next.

Here I find you have gone before me.

## 3 ※ The Days of Rest

Lord, surely goodness and mercy have pursued me all the days of my life and here I can find a dwelling place with you.

"Come all you who are weary" is your invitation and, Lord, I am walking the path that leads straight to your door. I am finding the comfiest couch in the corner and falling asleep.

I think of the saints who have gone on before me. The ones who worked the ground, who toiled and spent their days, and entered into their final rest with you, not to turn the ground on this earth again until you return. I tell my body and heart that I too will someday rest for eternity, and on this evening, in the cool of the day, I will practice that rest with you.

I will not strive to prove myself. I will not follow the voices that accuse me of having not done enough. I will turn down the volume on the world that tells me rest is for the weak. In fact, it's true. Rest is for the weak and we are all desperately so, and when we can finally admit that to one another, maybe we'll all be free.

In my surrender to rest, I admit that I couldn't do it all. There were plans that failed, entire beds overrun with weeds, hoped-for abundance that never arrived, days when I was too lazy to work harder and days I worked too hard and pulled out the roots of things I wanted. In this season of Sabbath, I realize another day of work does not equal another day of faithfulness. Remaining faithful to you requires me to admit that not everything produces year-round. Not the garden and not the busy hands of a believer. You have built dormancy into the rhythms of creation, and it is not a failure for us to do the same in our lives. Dormant branches, perennials, seeds, and bulbs. Dormant plans, productivity, list-making, and task-checking. Rest is your grace. Rest is an act of divine joy. Rest is a surrender to your rhythms and not my own.

Lord, send the snow, the cold, and the sleep. The harvest was plentiful. The songs of labor still fill my heart. We made it back home tired and raw, but we're here. You said it is finished, you said it is good, and so it is, in every way I can see.

## Cultivate

Father, yours is the earth and everything in it,
and that includes me (Psalm 24:1; 1 Corinthians 6:19–20).
You have set the sun and the stars in their boundaries (Psalm 74:16–17).
You command winter to quiet the earth (Job 37:6).
Help me to rest in the dormancy and stillness (Psalm 46:10),
and to so deeply root myself in you
so that I will yield fruit at the right time,
in the right season (Psalm 1:3).
Yours is the earth and everything in it, including me.

Consider writing your own winter prayer and find God's promises in Scripture as you pray.

4

# Counting the Seeds

*A man-made seed will never reproduce. An heirloom will continue to go on and on. A hardy heritage is not easily broken.*

"Kale seeds?" Madeleine, my daughter, gestures to the stalks of drying seed pods hanging from a basket on our porch. "Mom." She looks at me with that face. The one that reminds me that no one in this house actually enjoys kale, but I have managed to save thousands of seeds.

"If everything falls apart, at least we'll have kale to survive," I say as I add another few stems to the basket to dry. I've made this same comment to several friends and family members. No one is impressed. I believe one family member even said, "I would rather die." Yet there is something that keeps me going back to clip more seeds. Hoarding? Fear? Perhaps. But the act of collecting seeds from our own garden to save for future use is nothing short of miraculous to me. Seed husbandry is a field unto itself and I do what I can to dabble in it, preserving whatever seeds I can for next year's garden, for my neighbors, and for the apocalypse, apparently.

A few years ago, I traveled to Ireland with my mother and sister, and we visited an old garden outside of a convent where the nuns had been working the grounds for more than a hundred years. The grounds were extensive with flowers, perennials, herbs, and of course, a robust vegetable garden. The kale was nearly as tall as me. I couldn't help myself when I realized they sold heirloom seeds of all their varieties—kale, squash, bellflowers, leeks. I didn't want anything else to take home from Ireland. Just the seeds. Heirloom seeds carry a heritage within them. Someone has taken the time to collect seeds every year, preserving the variety through faithful husbandry, sacrificing the healthiest and most prolific crop to use for seed saving and not consumption. These seeds are hardy—they know how to grow the same thing. They're predictable. You get what you plant. (Don't try this with hybrid or GMO seeds. With hybrids, you could get either parent plant but never the repeat of what you initially grew. Some GMO seeds have been modified to never reproduce at all. It's not even possible.)

So when I planted the kale seeds from Ireland in my backyard garden, you can bet I was collecting every single seed that I could. The same variety that grew in Connemara was now growing in my humble patch, and I felt a sense of rootedness that this kind of heritage brings. A hardy heritage is not easily broken.

Every year I collect as many heirloom seeds from our garden

as I can. The best pumpkins get scooped and saved. Zinnia flower heads are gathered in paper bags. Cosmos, black beans, celosia, cockscomb, lupine, broccoli, gourds ... they all make their way into bags, bowls, baskets and wait for the long winter days where I'll sit and sort them. I'll spend our quiet, snowy afternoons separating the chaff from the seed. Occasionally I'll toss a small handful in the air, blow across my hand, and let the seeds fall. I'll use a fine mesh sieve and shake the seeds free from what encases them. Sometimes, I'll even grab a paintbrush to lightly brush the seeds apart from their casings on a small plate. This is the telltale sign of seed saving season. My flower farmer friend, Ashley, does the same and we share selfies with backs hunched over piles of seeds and paintbrushes in hand—a joyful way to say "it's seed saving time."

This is a patient work of endurance that won't amount to anything measurable today, but next year, the year after, maybe even in a hundred years, it will continue to produce a hardy heritage. It's more than just the vegetable or the flower. It's the story. It's the legacy of that seed. It's knowing that the tomato I'm eating today tastes so similar to the one that someone enjoyed back in 1942. It's the joy of displaying a pumpkin or gourd that shares the same appearance as some distant ancestor in County Mayo. It's knowing that the fragrant steam which rises from the sliced leeks and garlic sautéing in butter is the same scent that rose to the nostrils of men and women who have, for thousands of years now, stood over hot stoves, fires, and bubbling soups.

It's the heritage of those who have lived before me, whose names I may not know, but whose hands and husbandry brought this food to my table today.

There was a woman named Ruth Lee who lived across the street from my mother's house growing up. My mother remembers her as a sweet old woman who offered her and her eight siblings after-school snacks and a welcoming kitchen. Ruth Lee was a devout Christian, and my mother tells the story that years after she had grown, she learned from one of Ruth's family members how she used to pray for my mother and her family. She'd pray that my mother would know Jesus and that the grace of God would grip their hearts. It would be another twenty-plus years after my mother moved away from Ruth Lee's street before the Lord would awaken her heart in a country church hidden in the hills of upstate New York. But I like to believe, and I do believe, that I'm here because Ruth Lee prayed. Because one woman faithfully stewarded her hope and belief and planted that in the heart of my mother as a young child and teen, something real and true grew in my mother as well. The faith in Christ that Ruth Lee modeled for her was a heritage, an heirloom of faith, that grew and produced fruit.

That same heritage was lived out in front of me every day of my youth as my mother read her Bible at our breakfast table with the same mug of hot tea. Even when I would wake after she left for work, I would still find her Bible open from where she had been sitting hours before. The same heirloom seed planted in her was being planted in me. Someone long before Ruth Lee, someone whose name I will never know, stewarded that faith with care and passed it along. From generation to generation the gospel has persevered, and we are beneficiaries of those who did the work to preserve the seed. From the early church, to the nuns in Ireland, to the Ruth Lees, to the small patch of earth behind my house. We are all carrying the heirlooms within us in one way or another; let's pray these are the seeds that last.

## Cultivate

As you plan what seeds you're planting this year, consider what kind of seeds and source of seeds you want to plant. Do you want to be able to collect seeds and reuse them for another year? Not everyone wants to do this, but if you do, shop accordingly. Look around for local seed share programs in your area. Often there are other gardeners and farmers who would love to swap seeds. If it doesn't exist, consider starting your own. Connect with other local gardeners who love carrying on the heritage and husbandry of seeds. And if you cannot do any of the above, be like those who have gone before us—the early church, the nuns in Ireland, and Ruth Lee—and seek ways to carry on the good heritage we are given in Christ to the next generation.

# 5

# The Waiting Season

*The July garden begins in the January heart.*

*It's January*, which means it is time for the seed catalogues to start piling up on my desk. Each one a colorful contrast to the white and monochromatic landscape outside my window. They market spring and summer to me while I sit bundled in several blankets, a pair of fur-lined slippers, a beanie indoors, all while sitting next to my small faux-fireplace space heater. They are filled with pictures of luscious gardens, happy children frolicking with three-foot-long beans, storybook-sized pumpkins, and lettuce that would make any salad curmudgeon want to eat it.

January is when I am texting all of my gardening friends with desperate messages, begging for some encouragement or relief.

"It's not going to be winter forever, right?" I ask, knowing they have no respite for these subzero winds and days without sun. It's enough to make any soul despair. You don't think you have seasonal affective disorder until you finally see the sun after forty-five days and it makes you want to cry for joy. The garden feels like a cruel joke that someone told you once—the kind that takes fifteen minutes to tell, like the ones my brother-in-law tells, until the punchline is so groan-worthy, you wonder why you ever sat and listened at all. That's what the garden feels like in January. A distant, impossible thing.

In the north, if you're lucky enough, you might get a January thaw. That one day or two when the temperature rises above forty, the snow melts into a muddy tar pit, a few birds lilt on the branches, and everyone and their brother rides around with the windows down and Birkenstocks on their feet.

But even the January thaw isn't real.

Even the waiting gets weary.

So in January, I'm drawing long thin lines on the largest piece of paper I can find. I'm sketching my beds, notating where things were last year, and marking where they'll go this year. I'm shading out the garlic and shallot beds, where those bulbs are already sleeping. I'm drawing circles where the foxglove, roses, peonies, gypsophila, artichoke, lavender, salvia, motherwort, lupine, and all of our other perennial favorites will reemerge. I'm drawing tiny leaves and painting them green. I'm sketching celery tops and cabbage heads, delicately writing their names in ink next to each sketched bed.

January is when I stand at our seed cabinet and take a final seed inventory before submitting the last order. I've done everything from spreadsheets to handwritten lists, and in the end, it doesn't matter much because I still end up ordering too many packets of Zinnia and I always forget the herbs. The waiting isn't fatal to my love for gardening; it's fuel. The empty, cold earth and the emptying stores of my pantry remind me that the July garden needs to start now. The arm length zucchini needs to be remembered when the snow is still on the ground. The onions need a long winter runway. The rosemary too. If I want hot peppers in August, I have to think of hot peppers in January, when my salsa supply is halved and I have used up all of the jalapeños in the freezer.

The waiting produces something in the garden too.

We don't tend to wait well as a society. We want rapid results, microwave speed, filters to advance us, age us, or give us the answer we seek. We don't wait for much these days except that which is forced upon us. My mother used to tell me: "A watched pot never boils," but I find I can spend my days watching things, waiting for the boil, thinking my impatience will hasten the change. It's not so much the end result I'm looking for. I just want the time to pass while I am looking. Yet, how much we miss when we are watching the snow-drifted fields, waiting, without letting that time work its way within us.

And if we are not careful, if we do not wait with wisdom, we will find our hands empty when July comes. When the waiting ends, we will find that we have nothing but raw hands from wringing. If we're not careful, we risk digging up in snow the things that need a longer winter sleep. We will be left weeping, with bloody hands, begging for a sign of life long before its time.

When we wait, we join the ranks of every farmer, gardener, and land worker who stands at the edge of sleeping fields and sees the August waves of wheat. We join the lines of every kingdom believer who looks at a broken world and prays that harvest will come. We, as God's people, should be the most willing to wait for what is coming. We have our eyes fixed on Zion. We have eternity written in our hearts, waiting and longing for the redemption of creation; waiting and groaning for the full story to unfold into the magnificent final chapter. We are a waiting people. We long to see clearly—this beautiful mystery that he is slowly unfolding and revealing to us through the cross—that which looks like death is actually life. That which looks like defeat is a womb. We cannot get to the resurrection garden without walking by the "Place of the Skull" at Golgotha. Waiting for God's timing places us under his merciful, providential, perfect care.

And so we continue in this faithful work because we are God's people. We wait.

## Cultivate

It's time to plan. What will you grow this year? Where will it be planted? Use an empty journal page, stock up on the seed catalogs, the inspiring images online—start planning the garden. Make a list of what you already eat. What do you buy at the grocery store? Now you can plan to grow some of it. What are your favorite flowers? Every flower starts somewhere. Make a note to try and grow those. In the same way, we can do this for our hearts. Where do you want to see growth in your life? Where are you praying the Lord will bring fruit? Where do you want to invest in your life, your skills, your knowledge, your relationships, your home? The most vibrant gardens start in the darkest of winter. Here we eagerly wait.

6

# Hidden Friends

*In every stem and stalk sleeps an ally, a partner in good, a small winged or crawling friend who has just settled in for a long winter's nap.*

*I am not one* to scrape and rake the garden bare at the end of the season. In fact, if you were to drive by my home, you would see the haunting stalks of sunflowers, tomato plants, and zinnia stems, bent over; remnants of what was a vibrant life. I leave the majority of what remains at the end of the garden season for the spring. The winter will dehydrate them completely, turning what feels an impossible task of uprooting in the fall into an easy work of cut, rake, and toss in the spring. What happens in these hidden places is almost like a page out of a storybook. I leave the sunflower heads for the birds who will gather the last of their winter seeds here, and in doing so, will plant the hundreds of sunflower volunteers I'll have next spring. The now hollowed out stalks and stems can stay.

Garden-friendly critters will crawl inside and nest. The jumping spiders wrap themselves in white webs and tuck in for the winter. The praying mantis egg sacs, brown and tough, are filled with almost two hundred eggs (of which only a few will survive) and they make their winter home along the woody stems of the plants, and inside the greenhouse frame and door. Bumblebees, beneficial beetles, dragonflies, and other friendly spiders are all taking a long winter's nap here. Let them rest. I'll leave the stalks and stems until the winter ends, giving them all a chance to wake up.

I feel a kind of winter solidarity when the gates won't open for the piles of snow and the beds are buried beneath the white, yet I can see the stems still sticking out of the surface. I know, in those narrow spaces, the friends who will help make that garden a better place are sleeping and waiting. I've given them a home, shelter, a place to burrow in and give new life. While I'm stirring another pot of soup in mid-February, I look to the empty square footage of the potager and remember that this gardening is not just a work that I do. It is the work of the jumping spider in spring, the bumblebee queen who emerges alone and seeks a new home as she bounces along the early spring motherwort, the work of the praying mantis who captures the bugs that seek to destroy my plants. I cannot explain to you what joy this is, but I cheerfully greet the first wolf spider of spring who crawls out from the dirt as I plant.

"Ah, we made it," I might whisper. "Happy hunting!"

*Ah, we made it.* Isn't this what we all seem to say after the long seasons of waiting? It's the first sign of life as a robin flits near my window, asking again for more seeds. It's the sunflowers that the goldfinches planted in October that sprout to life before I've even had a chance to clear the beds. It's the jumping spiders that hitch a ride on a seed tray into my growing room inside. It's the way my neighbor returns to his front yard after a long winter and waves to us from his driveway. It's the way the grass goes from the sorry brown to the spring green. *Ah, we made it,* is the familiar anthem of spring, and I want to give every person, creature, and small helpful friend who visits this humble plot of ground a place to say it with me. We made it. There is a place for us here. Hospitality doesn't just show up in my kitchen and living room; it makes its way into my garden as well. You never know who you're ministering to through sharing your home. The least of these look road weary, as if their souls may not survive another winter. So don't clean up. Don't worry about how the house looks. Carve out a space in the middle of the mess for someone to lay their weary head. Watch what the garden can teach you about your home.

> So leave the stems, the stalks, the twigs
> Leave the rusty autumn leaves
> It all can wait 'til spring arrives
> You'll see the garden as it yawns alive
>
> The places that are dark and small
> Cradle, protect, and cover all
> The critters that sleep: from spiders to bees,
> Hospitable gardening for the least of these

## Cultivate

Don't be too eager to clean out your garden beds. Let some things stand and wait until spring for a true clean up. Instead, invite some friends and neighbors to a winter meal. Open your home. Carve out a space for some weary winter hearts. Light the candles, spread out blankets on the back of your couches, play some good music. Give a hearty cheer of gospel hope—*it is finished. We made it.*

If you must do some end of season clean up, consider what you want for your garden next year. Provide nutrients for the winter, compost to decompose what remains of the leaf piles, and create some covering for the perennial plants and bugs that will cheerfully greet you in the spring.

7

# The Winter Table

*Diligent hands in summer feed the table in winter.*

$B$*ags of onions* hang in our basement stairwell. Cabbages are piled in a basket in the corner. The shelves are full of everything we could possibly preserve: peppers, cucumbers, jams, sauces, salsa, dried fruits, sage, rosemary, thyme, chamomile, and lavender. Hundreds of heads of garlic hang from the walls of my kitchen. Potatoes and sweet potatoes are in the basket below the island. Butternut squash and acorn squash line the back of my kitchen counters. Strawflowers, statice, eucalyptus, poppy seed pods, they all hang upside down, drying in bursts of shape, color, and texture. The freezer is full of everything I did not can: green beans, jalapenos, celery, sweet peppers, zucchini, spinach, corn, basil, and more. The garden might be put to bed, but it has poured into my kitchen and it is wide awake through my senses. Our December to March meals will revolve around this stock.

But all of this food doesn't just appear. The table we're feasting at started last January when I planned it all out. It happened in March when I started seeds beneath eerily purple grow lights in our utility room. It happened in June when I weeded in a light rain until my back ached. It happened in July when I pruned the things that were painful to prune. It happened in August when I woke early to harvest and hung the onions in the barn rafters to cure.

It happened in October when I tied and hung the remaining herbs to dry.

Diligent hands in summer feed the table in winter.

They make our Thanksgiving dishes of sweet potato casserole, stuffing with garden vegetables, mashed potatoes still stained with the dirt of my field, green beans my children picked that are fried in the garlic and onions we will be eating all winter long.

Diligent hands in summer make our December desserts with berries from June and August, and provide the dried flowers and herbs that are tucked into the Christmas gift wrapping.

Diligent hands in summer feed us in mid-January with salsa that still tastes fresh.

In February, I cover our table centerpiece with dried strawflowers we picked in October. Bright straw-like blooms of red, pink, orange, and white. Reminders that beauty grew here once and it will again.

Diligent hands fill our table in the dead of winter, when the garden feels like a distant memory and we begin to forget how to hope. I don't do it for bragging rights or any kind of food or garden superiority. I am very much aware that we can go to the grocery store up the road and buy up any vegetable or flower that we could want. Part of why I garden is to provide something to our home and to teach something to our children. There is value in working hard when the payout might not come for months and months. There is value in working hard for a harvest when the harvest itself might not be measurably remarkable to anyone but yourself. There is value in work, period.

This is the same thing we learn when we pour into the lives of those we love and see no fruit. Lord, is this work worth doing? When we give our time and our prayers into places and situations that seem hopeless. Lord, do diligent hands produce fruit even there? In seasons when we have bountiful harvests, we forget that some of that fruit won't really be seen, enjoyed, or even ready until long after we've celebrated the harvest. In seasons of stark winters, we might even find that the things the Lord stored up in us during seasons of life are there for us to finally enjoy, to finally understand, to finally feast on. It's hard to fully grasp the sovereignty of God until we are in a season where we need to see that he's in control. It's hard to fully celebrate the mercy of God until we are in a season where we desperately need his mercy. It's hard to feast at the table of suffering and sorrow until we see that even there, he has prepared a table for us in the presence of our enemies. The diligent hands of the Father are always working in us, in both the summer and the winter. The diligent hands of our own faith are working, albeit in broken ways, by the direction of the Spirit, to teach us what we need to store up on and save for the dead of winter.

Lord, teach me to store up. Preserve in me that which I'll need when I've lost hope. When the nights are long. When the days are cold. Teach me to remain.

> Summer and winter, springtime and harvest,
> Sun, moon and stars in their courses above
> Join with all nature in manifold witness
> To Thy great faithfulness, mercy and love.[1]

## Cultivate

One of our favorite winter meals is a pot of soup, fresh bread with butter dripping, and jam that we pull off the shelf from our summer harvest. This type of meal, a soup filled with vegetables and whatever meat is on hand, is on weekly rotation at our home and I'd encourage you to do the same. Here's one recipe that frequents our table once the temperatures begin to drop. It's a comfort food and it's sure to warm the bellies of everyone who gathers at your table. Fair warning, this soup is not for the waistline conscious. (While I'm sure alterations or replacements can be made, I find that the joy of eating something so deliciously creamy in the bleak midwinter is a true boost to the spirits.) Enjoy it heartily as a mid-winter feast.

*Creamy Chicken Gnocchi and Vegetable Soup*
Serves 8–10

### CHICKEN PREP

- ½ c. salted butter
- 6–10 chicken thighs, chopped into bite size pieces
- dried or fresh herbs such as sage, thyme, oregano
- 1 tsp. cumin
- 1 tsp. paprika
- Salt and pepper to taste

### MAIN DUTCH OVEN PREP

- 6 bacon slices
- 4–6 garlic cloves, peeled and minced
- 1 large onion, peeled and chopped
- 3–4 ribs of celery, chopped (about 1 c.)
- 4 whole carrots, chopped
- 6 small potatoes, chopped into bite-sized cubes
- ½ c. salted butter
- ½ c. flour
- 1 c. milk, preferably 2% or more

- 1 c. heavy cream (or 2 c. heavy cream, depending on how indulgent you want this soup to be)
- 8–10 cups of chicken broth (to desirable thickness of soup)
- 1 c. chopped broccoli, peas, corn, spinach, kale, or whatever other vegetables you enjoy
- ½ c. parmesan cheese
- 2 cups of gnocchi (fresh or dried), however much you would enjoy. We like to add enough so that every bite has a gnocchi in it.
- Salt and pepper to taste (generously salt this dish throughout cooking)

### STEPS

1. Sauté the chicken separately in ½ stick of butter (¼ c.) or olive oil. Season generously with salt, pepper, oregano, sage, cumin, paprika. Feel free to experiment here with different seasonings, but just don't cook the chicken without any seasoning! Once the chicken is cooked through, set aside.

2. Heat a large Dutch oven on the stovetop. Fry the bacon slices until they're crispy. Remove from the pot, but keep the bacon fat simmering on the bottom.

Keep the bacon to crush and sprinkle on top of your soup!

3. Sauté the garlic and onions in the bacon grease. If necessary, add a bit of butter. Salt the garlic and onions (a sprinkle or dash will do).

4. Once the onions are translucent and the garlic is aromatic, add the celery and carrots. Stir over medium heat for about 5–7 minutes or until the celery and carrots are slightly soft or browned.

5. Add the potatoes to the pan and continue to sauté. (Add an additional sprinkle or dash of salt again.) If you want to add more vegetables from your garden, now is the time! Add whatever you'd like to veggie-up the soup. Additionally, you can wait until just before adding the milk and cream to add vegetables that won't hold up for as long such as broccoli or peas.

6. Once the vegetables seem to be well-browned, add ½ of the butter to the bottom of the pan. I usually make a small circle in the center. Once the butter is melted, stir the vegetables in and immediately add the ½ c. of flour. Stir until all of the vegetables are covered.

7. Add the chopped, cooked chicken. Stir all together. Add more salt and seasoning if necessary. If you're

enjoying a glass of wine while you cook, now is a fun time to splash some into the pan. A hint of white wine would be lovely in this soup.

8. Pour in chicken broth. (Water would work as well, but consider adding bouillon or be prepared to offset the flavor loss with more herbs.)

9. Bring to a boil, stirring frequently to make sure the roux isn't sticking to the bottom of the pan but is blending well into the broth. Keep at a low simmering boil for at least 20 minutes. If too much liquid cooks off or the soup thickens too rapidly, add more liquid.

10. Once the soup is thickened and simmers for a while, add the milk, heavy cream, and parmesan. Stir over med-low heat until the soup thickens.

11. Add the gnocchi and let it sit at med-low for about 10 minutes before serving.

### Additional Recipe Options

- 1 c. cheddar or gouda cheese
- Crush the bacon from step 1
- Fresh parsley to sprinkle
- Buffalo sauce to make this taste a bit like my home territory
- Crushed red peppers to spice it up

Serve with warm bread, good butter (think Kerrygold salted butter) and a summer jam (we usually pull out raspberry lime, blueberry, concord grape, or strawberry).

8

# Hidden in Winter

*Do not weep, for she is not dead but sleeping.*

*The first snow* has buried the last of my winter greens and carrots. A little bit of digging, making my fingers raw and icy, reveals the carrots are still there. The kale and mizuna too. Sweeter for the snow. This blanketing of snow early in the season is not yet as damaging as some of the later snows. But it certainly covers what remains. These beds, which were roaring with life just a short six months ago are now silent, not even a slight breath from their bones. I check on the small plants in the cold frame—some eucalyptus I'm trying to overwinter, radishes, onions still going strong. Some hardy stock flower still blooms inside of the now white ceiling of the greenhouse. Some last leeks, brussels, broccoli, lettuce—they all poke quietly out from the white. Final vestiges of our July planting for the fall garden. Some gardeners I know are still going full throttle this time of year. Their cold frames are filled and warmed by the sun, and they'll continue to harvest for weeks or months to come. Maybe that's you, and if it is, you have my utmost respect. I get to this time of year and I am just flat out done. Spent. The garden has emptied every last reserve of energy I had, and I long to be covered over—silent—resting for a season.

Will anything return from this utter exhaustion? As for myself, I feel unsure. Between the wrap-up of the garden, the holidays, and the grit in my soul needed to face winter, I am not convinced there is much worth betting on. I am wilting and weary. I long to go dormant. Just let me be forgotten for a few months until I wake up again.

There is a special gift that comes in the times of dormancy: visibility. Suddenly, the gardener can see where the plant is dead, where it has branched in the wrong direction, and where pruning needs to occur. Without the green foliage and vibrant signs of life, the gardener can tend to the more tender things such as shape, health, and where the energy of the plant will go. While plants sleep, the gardener tends. While the ground freezes and the roots hibernate, the skeleton view of the garden and all of its spaces are in full view. It is a blank canvas of possibility. But don't be fooled; things are not as dead as they seem.

This is what I feel I need to shout about my own soul in the depths of dormant seasons. Don't be fooled! She's not dead! She is only sleeping.

Everything is hidden now,
asleep for the long night
'til the bell rings from the east
that blessed morning light.

Lifeblood stilled, veins stiff in place
no flowering bloom to hold.
Black and terse, each branch is caught
mid-stretch seized by the cold.

Everything is silent now
and so shall we all be.
Buried, covered, waiting for
the trumpet of the spring.

## Cultivate

Use this opportunity to reassess your perennials, your hedges, bushes, and garden beds. Think about where you might want to plant perennials next season, sketch out garden ideas, and use the blank canvas of winter as an opportunity to think about what you want to change and edit on your property. It's a good time to go out and purchase some new houseplants or refresh the houseplants already in your home. Update your soil and pots, give plant baths, move things around, and refresh the interior of your house while everything sleeps outside.

Houseplants love a good bath or shower, and this is the time of year to do it. Bring your plants into your bathtub or shower, setting them all side by side. Get the water temperature to a nice warm temperature, but not too hot. Think rainforest: this is the atmosphere you want in your bathroom. Run the shower over them for a good ten to thirty minutes and watch as the soil rehydrates and the tiny little bugs float out; then take a few minutes to wash both the top and bottoms of the leaves. Wipe off the dust with a microfiber cloth and your plant will be as happy as a new seedling in spring. In some cases, your plants might need fresh soil. This is a good time to repot plants, add or replace soil, move them to larger pots, and take care of your indoor houseplants that serve your home all year round.

## 9

# The Empty Season

*Feast, and your halls are crowded.*
*Fast, and the world goes by.*
*Succeed and give, and it helps you live.*
*But no man can help you die.*

*I wrote a story* when I was in high school—my own "Greek" myth. It was the story of a young girl who lost her love and sought for him in the middle of a dark winter. She would sing into the wind in hopes her song would make him return. The melody turned to mourning as she howled every night. Her true love would never return. To this day, my story said, she still sings in the wind, reminding us of the love she lost in the bitter winter.

I think of that story when I cut the last of the garlic from the clusters hanging in the kitchen, pour out the remaining peas, and slice the final few shallots.

I have used the last of nearly everything. Soon there will be nothing to show for my work. Soon the garden will be nothing more than a haunting song on the winds that holler at my door.

When I use the last of these things, the song carries on the loss of what was. Dug out and poured out. Those hot, sweat-drenched days feel so far off. I can't remember the smell of dirt, the feel of hard work trailing down my neck, the sun that beat down on my pale skin. Did I work as hard as I could have? How much did I waste?

The windows on our porch swirl with frost and the wind seals us in. I stand on our frigid porch to listen to the soprano notes as the snow whips into stiff peaks and drifts, covering the places we just shoveled. The chickens huddle together on the roosting bars. In the mornings, one of us has to shuffle out through the snow to break the ice on the surface of the chicken water, despite there being a heater running underneath it all night. We haven't seen the barn cat in days.

We are nothing more than slaves to winter at this point. The air is harsh, and I wonder if our roots will last.

What do we do when it seems all of the places we poured our heart into have withered and disappeared? When the storehouses, pantry shelves, and baskets of stock are nothing more than clutter covered with cobweb dust?

What do we do when the relationship we poured our life into for twenty years stops abruptly because someone walks out the door? When the adult child you've given your life to decides, overnight, that they no longer believe what you have raised them to believe?

When the church dwindles, the work doesn't seem to make a difference, cancer still kills, marriages still fail, and people still die? What do we do when the wind is just a reminder of mourning?

What do we do when winter is harsh and empty? Even the most optimistic gardener might find herself harmonizing with the wind's song.

If I'm being honest, most days when I feel this, I want to go to sleep. It's all too heavy and bleak to carry. I think if the prophet Elijah could be worn out from all of the work and lack of fruit, and weary enough to need God to tell him to take a nap and eat, then perhaps it's OK if the winter slump nudges me to do the same.

But if we're kingdom-minded people, I suppose it looks a lot like the Saturday between Friday and Sunday. A faithful plodding on, even when the day is just as dark as the night. In C. S. Lewis's classic work *The Screwtape Letters*, Screwtape writes to Wormwood about the one who follows the "Enemy" (who is in fact, God)—"Do not be deceived, Wormwood. Our cause is never more in danger than when a human, no longer desiring, but still intending, to do our Enemy's will, looks round upon a universe from which every trace of Him seems to have vanished, and asks why he has been forsaken, and still obeys."

I've walked there and know people right now who are faithfully plodding on even though they'd be the first to tell you they don't know where God is. Or perhaps they know where he is, but the days feel cold and dark. Even here, in the shadowed places where it feels like the sun is no longer shining, he is with us. We cannot fear. We cannot look at our emptiness and think it means that we have nothing. It's after the wind stops her mournful song, and I emerge from my cocoon of flannel sheets that I remember the true sound of a winter night. The snow crunches under my boots, the surface of icy snow glitters under the moonlight, and the earth is muted, except for the distant sound of a great-horned owl somewhere deep in the woods.

Somewhere far below my steps, the garden sleeps. Keep going. All is not lost.

## Cultivate

This is the time of year to collect seed catalogs and gardening books and fill your margins with plans. Get some graphing paper and sketch out your next garden. Plan out some new ideas. I like to plan ahead where I'm getting my seeds and scout out prices. When there is a vacuum of space, an empty place, fill it with the plans of life. You can begin to push back against the darkness right now, before your hands even reach into the dirt. All beautiful and prolific gardens begin in the heart of the empty-handed winter gardener.

> Lord, here in this hollow and empty place,
> I look around for a sign of your face
> but you have vanished from the warmth of my hands
> I am swallowed up in shadows in this barren land
>
> The night feels dark and cold, too long
> for me to learn how to sing a louder song

so I'm crawling deeper in to the cave
Once you laid in a tomb and did the same

Help me to trust you when the night is dark
Help me to obey when the winds howl
Help me to keep going when the drifts pile high
Help me to rest when I cannot see where I'm going next

And Father, please shine a light into this night
Make my darkness like the noon of day
Scatter the things that linger in the shadows
Send them running so I can see what they are
Let nothing remain hidden from you
And in this, crack the tomb of my heart
Help me to see that emptiness is certainly not nothing

> If I say, "Surely the darkness shall cover me,
>     and the light about me be night,"
> even the darkness is not dark to you;
>     the night is bright as the day,
> for darkness is as light with you. (Psalm 139:11–12)

10

# Grief

*And the past is the past, and that is what time means,*
*and time itself is one more name for death.*

*I can remember the summers* of my childhood. My mother scattering the hillsides with flowers. The raspberry patch just to the southeast of the goldfish-stocked pond. The vegetable garden my father planted with me in the hard-as-rock clay soil. The way he looked with the rototiller in our front lawn. The way that first green bean tasted. The farmer up the road who sold sweet corn. The Barbers' farm stand on the other side of town, always stocked with whatever vegetable you could want.

I would fill my pockets with a few quarters and a carrot or two and walk the half mile to the corner store in the center of our tiny town. On the way, I'd pass the neighbor horses, feeding them whatever carrots and snacks I managed to squirrel away in my pockets. The dust of the road would kick up behind me and I'd eventually make my way to the store, fill a paper lunch bag with candy, and slowly meander back, via the creek, to home. Home was the blue house on the hill. It was on the other side of "the queen's staircase," as I called the fallen stonewall that climbed the hillside. The driveway was lined with blackberries and the pine trees my father had planted twenty years before. The sounds of the creek would wake me in the mornings, rushing through the valley after a strong rain.

It's all a blurry, glossy memory to me now. I can never go back.

Years ago, a hurricane ravaged through that very valley, wiping out some of the familiar roads and places I knew so well. Recently my mother informed me that despite all of the repairs on the banks of that creek, the damage was too severe, causing the road that I grew up on to begin collapsing into the water.

"They're talking about buying the two houses that remain on that side of the road," she said. One of those was mine.

"So they'll just stay ... empty?" I imagined the large blue house, alone in the woods, empty and abandoned, left there for teenage kids to vandalize and desecrate. The perennial flowers ripped out. The place where my first garden was overgrown with weeds and sycamore. "I guess so," she said. "The whole hillside is just washing away."

I suppose this is the closest description I can give you of grief. The very place that was once your safety is empty. You can never go back.

I feel the ache of never being able to go back in the dead of winter. I'm nearly forty, so if my calculations are somewhat correct,

I might only have another forty to fifty gardens left to plant. And that's generous, if age doesn't wipe me out. If the roads don't cave in on my hands, my back, my knees, my mind. For all I know, I might only have twenty.

Only a few more chances to figure out how to grow David Austin roses.

Only a few more summers to grow the kind of tomatoes that make you understand why people love tomatoes.

Only a few more pink and gold sunsets behind rows of corn.

And if I really want to make it sting—only about four more summers to grow zinnia, lavender, pineapple sage, and edelweiss with my daughter before she is ready to leave this home behind her. Only eleven more summers to grow the best pumpkin with my son.

We can never go back.

The summer has closed behind us. What lies before us feels like grief waiting to happen. As much as we're looking forward to it, that too will end. The roads will close. The houses will fall empty. Even our gardens will become overgrown.

We will taste death like the gall it is. Bitter, empty, hollow. It will scream in our bones like the winter winds. I remember broom corn touching the sky and my son running beneath it and feel the memories fade just out of view. I remember my daughter, small and in the rows of the garden, too young to know that life is not forever and this too feels like a door I cannot open again. A house of memories on a hill that is washing away.

We can never go back.

## Cultivate

Pray Psalm 103:13–18:

> As a father shows compassion to his children,
>> so the LORD shows compassion to those who fear him.

Lord, thank you for your compassion. This world is heavy, brief, dark, and cold. Thank you for remembering us.

> For he knows our frame;
>> he remembers that we are dust.

Lord, my frame is wasting away with each day. I cannot outrun death. I cannot breathe life into dust. You give and you take away.

> As for man, his days are like grass;
>> he flourishes like a flower of the field;

Lord, time is like sand in my fingers. It's the buried grass beneath the snow. It's brief, temporary, and small.

> for the wind passes over it, and it is gone,
>> and its place knows it no more.

Lord, the winter winds stir around me and I know that I cannot go back to where I was. Even the places I once stood don't remember me. Someday my name might be forgotten. Except for you. You, Lord, remember me.

> But the steadfast love of the LORD is from everlasting
> to everlasting on those who fear him,
> > and his righteousness to children's children,

Lord, as the waters of this world erase the places I used to call home, help me to make my home in you. You are immovable, indestructible, and safe.

> to those who keep his covenant
> > and remember to do his commandments.

Lord, as you remember me in these days of grief, help me to remember you.

# 11

# The Days of Dark

*Help me, protect me in the moving sea*
*until I reach the shore of unceasing praise.*

*There are some mornings* I cannot bring myself to move. It's 8 a.m. and somehow the sun hasn't split the sky yet. It lies hidden in a southern valley, somewhere beyond the clouds that hang low. Morning may be here but somehow it is still gray. The sun is a literal ball of fire and somehow it is still cold. The days are brief, and temperatures linger in the single digits.

Every year around this time, the time of my birthday, I have this haunting thought: every year, we pass the anniversary of our own death. Once every year, without fanfare or warning, I live the ordinary, normal life that I have, not knowing that it is the calendar date on which I will someday die. I know it's dark. It's not something I dwell on for long, but on cold nights and icy mornings, the days when the soul of life feels distant and beauty doesn't linger in the doorway, I think about such things. In his famous musical *Hamilton*, Lin Manuel-Miranda's main character, Alexander Hamilton sings: "I imagine death so much it feels more like a memory."[2] This lyric felt like an old friend the first time I heard it.

I wonder if I will fall asleep in one breath and, with the next, wake up in the kingdom, face to face with Jesus.

I wonder what books will be left unread? I wonder what plans will remain unfulfilled? What garden beds will lay dormant? On the coldest mornings, I roll toward the warmth of my husband, tucking my cold feet into his legs. I wonder which one of us will have to say goodbye first. I listen for the gentle strumming of his heart; the rise and fall of his breath.

*Memento mori.* Remember that you will die. As someone who spends a great deal of her life thinking about how to make things come to life—children, love, the garden—it's a sharp slice to my heart to remember that all things will die. Of course, I have seen this firsthand in the garden. In the animals we raise. In the family and friends I love. The gray hairs have only multiplied on my husband's beard and brow. Our border collie, Violet, used to play with limitless energy in the winter, pulling Madeleine around on a plastic sled with the rope in her mouth as our girl hollered and laughed. Now our old dog limps and takes her time to go up the stairs, and even she has white hairs accumulating around her eyes.

To be acquainted with death is to be acquainted with darkness. Death wants to swallow all things whole, into a place that feels like a waking nightmare and a faint dream. Death rattles in the lungs and against the cage of our heart, and we all know it is the shadow behind every nostalgic memory, every hopeful endeavor, every bountiful harvest. We are all singing but death wants to steal the song from our lips.

The fig leaves have fallen off the tree. It sleeps in dormancy by our south facing window. There is nothing left to harvest, and it is not nearly time to plant.

The days are short and life echoes this in its brevity. Another funeral, another tragic accident, another terminal illness. Another reminder that the day I die will fit somewhere in these squared-off black and white calendar days. On these gray days, I can feel the walls closing in around us. The headlines seem more grim. The collective mood of society seems more entrenched in despair than I remember. The ache of a world waiting for redemption is at my fingertips every day, and I have spent more times in prayer just saying "Lord, help" and "Lord, come soon" than I can recall. It's all too dark. Abuse, starvation, corruption, murder, war, hatred, more true crime podcasts than we know what to do with, more things to be outraged over than we know how to feel outrage.

Another pastor who can't be trusted.

Another mass shooting leaving grieving parents with empty arms.

Another disease that cannot be cured.

Another war that decimates a generation of women and children.

Darkness oozing around me like a pool of black ink, slowly staining what remains of us. The gray hairs of death touching everything I see.

And yet—the amaryllis blooms tall and red at the center of the table. The paperwhites reach for the sun. The lime tree and lemon tree have flowers and fruit on them. For Christmas, I sliced our four limes, squeezing them into glasses for drinks, their citrus burst nearly lighting my senses on fire. By some gift of grace, our dinners are meals still served from the garden. The roasted potatoes, onions simmering in butter, herbs in the pan with the steak. Little flickers of light in a dark world. Songs that persist even when the walls close in. Lanterns of hope swinging in a dark night. And so we fill our windows with candlelight, we remember that we will die, and then we squeeze the bursting joy out of life while we can. *Memento mori.* And the bursting hope that Christ has come and will come again. Both of these. Even in the dark.

## Cultivate

Consider cultivating a winter garden. Purchase citrus trees that are hardy in your zone and keep them in pots where you live. Grow some vibrant indoor plants and watch how they reach for the sunlight. Buy bouquets at the grocery store. Snag those winter flowers when they go on sale. Grow herbs on your windowsill and cut from them all winter long. Plant a monstera and let it climb and stretch all over your living room. Get outside and get sunlight when the sky is finally blue. Be committed to life where life can be found. Do not despair.

Father, when I walk through the valleys of the shadow of death, when the lingering dark feels longer than I can handle,

*Winter*

help me to remember that you are my shepherd
and there is no shadow that passes my door
that did not first pass yours.

## 12

# The Lonely Season

*No one knows loneliness like winter.*

*T*he gate of the garden is now sealed shut by the snow.
I'd have to dig to find it,
the iced-over lock,
the solid hinges now unturned.

The snow drifts are taller than my hips,
whispering winds whipping them up into white caps,
beautiful and final,
creation's own gate closed against the paths I want to walk.

Here I stand at the edge of a plowed driveway
where the stone turns to snow. Rock solid.
I cannot find the paths anymore.
They belong to others now,
small and winter-deft,

*Winter*

but they no longer belong to me.
Not in this season.

No one knows loneliness like winter.

With her howling winds and heavy clouds,
her gray days without sun,
her tree-branch fingertips scratching at an empty sky,
She who writes poetry against the windows,
yet no one stays long enough to listen or read.
We all raise our fists at winter,
and no one knows her name.

I'm at the edge of where the grass should start,
but winter has consumed everything in her wake,

leaving just me.

I feel this yawning absence deep in my bones,
the very core of me slowing down to a whispering echo:

I am alone.
A hollowed out wind rushes in,
that familiar fear that numbs my lips,
*Am I this easily forgotten and erased?*

I know that my God who made the summer sun
   and flourishing vine,
also ordains the cold and the ice.
The God who spun creation in this wild dance,

## 12 ❄ The Lonely Season

placing the stars in that great expanse,
also rested on the seventh day.

Alone, in joy, the Trinity.
Content in three, the silence grand.
God, who made the seas and land
ordained the silence of the snow
that puts to sleep the things that grow.

So while my soul, my heart, my fingers, and my breath
feel utterly and completely and devastatingly
alone,
where even the garden gate is closed
to all of my hopes and plans,
I listen to the swirling wind as she sings:
*Glory, glory, glory to the God who makes me sing.*
I listen to the trees as they reach, empty-handed:
*Glory, glory, glory to the God who fills our veins.*
I listen to the clouds as they cover:
*Glory, glory, glory to the God who covers you.*
And I listen to the cold:
*Glory, glory, glory to the God who doesn't leave us alone.*

### Cultivate

Find a frosted window today. See the way the moisture paints a picture of beauty. Try to capture this scene somehow through a photograph, a sketch, a painting. Even in the empty season, the quiet beauty reveals the Lord's kindness. His work continues to point to him, even on the frozen panes. If you cannot find the beauty in the lonely places, seek to find places where you can bring beauty and relief to someone else's loneliness. Visit a nursing home, a house-bound church member, an elderly friend or relative. Where winter wants to lure you into seclusion, be an active representation of God's nearness and remembering in this season.

## 13

# The Dark and Tender Season

*We must be tender with all budding things,*
*Our Maker let no thought of Calvary*
*Trouble the morning stars in their first song.*

*It's seed starting season*, which means I'm counting down the weeks until the last frost. My children understand this as I write a large "7" on the chalkboard.

"Seven weeks until the last frost?" Madeleine asks and I nod. This is the season when it all starts to move toward life again. Of course, we know life has always been there, one way or another, but this is where it really starts to filter into every plan, weekend, and forecast.

The purple grow lights give off an alien glow in our utility room, and the onions, celery, and rosemary I started a few weeks ago have already broken through.

"Good morning," I whisper to the green stems that unfold from the soil. The seed case is spent. These onions will reach maturity in about six months. I'll hang them from the beams in our barn and we'll enjoy them all winter. They will be salsa and seasoning, fajitas and soup base. But today they are just waking up. They are not yet ready to talk about the things they will be. They're not ready yet to be cut, thinned, cured, chopped.

This is the way of the tenderness of spring. The tenderness of a seed that has just found its roots. It needs water, light, the encouraging presence of a gardener who is patient.

Here in this disrupted dirt, I stand watch over the seed I planted. I do not expect it to mature before it's time. There is no pressure for it to produce ahead of schedule. It's a seed and it will grow, no doubt. There's also still plenty of time for it to fail. But I'm going to patiently see it through this tenderness, for both my sake and for the seedlings'.

All seeds start in the dark. Most of them don't even need light to germinate. If you can picture it, these small, sometimes barely-visible-to-the-naked-eye seeds don't really need our human help. This magical (and to be honest, very scientific) thing called gravitropism occurs, the seed senses gravity and the direction to grow, the perfect balance of moisture and nutrients and time dance together in a small symphony in the dark, telling the seed to grow. Everything it needs to become the final plant is already written inside of that tiny little shell. What kind of flower, how tall it can be, the hue of blue, the bend of the pod—it's all there. There in the dark, it unfolds and reaches toward the surface, where inevitably, if all goes to plan, the light waits.

This is where I find that the Lord sees even the smallest seed, even the one that he is faithfully, tenderly working within me. If it starts in the dark, then even I am sometimes surprised to find that this thing is growing—this conviction, this love, this desire for more of him, this answer to my pain or suffering, this ability to see where he wants me to go, this deep sense of gravitropism in my own soul. The roots go deep, the seed unfurls, and here we are cradling this tender shoot that he has called forth. Or maybe we simply are the tender seedling. Every inch of our soul feels new, raw, easily broken, trying to figure out how to simply be alive. It's a surprising and reassuring thing to emerge from the dark only to see that the darkness was the plan all along. That's where things needed to start. Maybe we're not quite ready or able to know what the plan is or where this final tender seedling will eventually end up. Maybe our souls are still aching a bit from this thing that needs to find the light.

Maybe it was in the dark that we prayed and thought nothing happened. In the dark, we asked and waited, feeling only gravity, not realizing that pull was the very thing cracking us open. Maybe in the dark, we couldn't see the light, still calling.

The Lord does his best work in the dark, or at least that is what I tell myself when I am feeling the tight squeeze of a buried prayer. Before there was light, God said: "I AM." Before there was resurrection, he was. Before there was new life, he was. There in the dark expanse of the universe, there in the darkness of the tomb, there in the darkness of each womb, and here in the dark of the earth I've dug my soul into. The Lord has written it all. Hope begins in the dark.

## Cultivate

This is the time of year to start seeds. You'll want to take the time to find out your zone and see when the estimated last frost date is. This date isn't fixed in stone but thanks to relatively predictable weather patterns, it's very reliable. Make a list of what you want to grow this year. See what grows best in your gardening zone. Pick a few seeds that need to be started indoors (tomatoes, peppers, cabbage, broccoli, etc.) Find a sunny windowsill or get some grow lights, a few bags of soil, some cell trays from your local store, and get started. Remind yourself as you sow the seeds that the General Revelation can be seen here—God's creation shows us what he's doing. A seed, planted in the dark, almost looks forgotten. But you and I both know it's not. All seeds start in the dark.

Pray this breath prayer:

> For as the rain and the snow come down from heaven
> and do not return there but water the earth,
> making it bring forth and sprout,
> giving seed to the sower and bread to the eater,
> so shall my word be that goes out from my mouth;
> it shall not return to me empty,
> but it shall accomplish that which I purpose,
> and shall succeed in the thing for which I sent it.
>
> (Isaiah 55:10–11)

## 13 ❧ The Dark and Tender Season

Inhale: *The word that goes out from Your mouth,*
Exhale: *shall not return to You empty.*

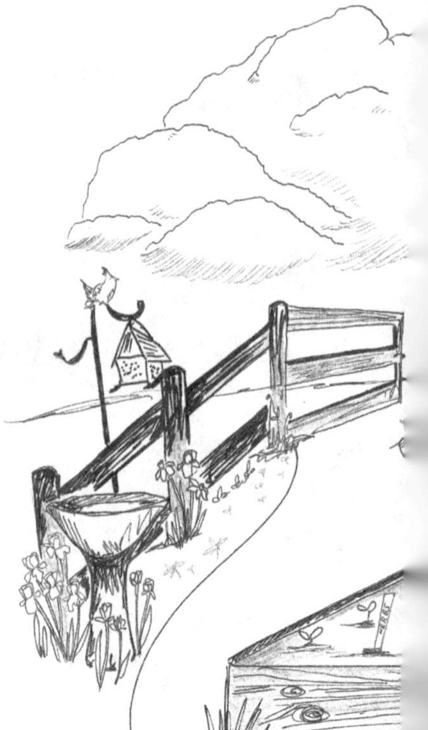

# SPRING

14

# The Late Snow

*You have fixed all the boundaries of the earth;*
*you have made summer and winter.*

*It's the middle* of March and we woke up—again—to a blanket of snow. Not just a dusting but a legitimate eight to ten inches. Wind is whipping up the snow devils in the fields and any sign of life has retreated back inside its burrow. Our normal visits from our barn cat, Finn, have stopped. He's surely nestled inside of a barn loft with whatever old blankets or hay bales remain there. The birds have gone silent. A few stray deer trails wander across the neighbor's back meadow, but that's it. It feels like all of our spring hopes died overnight. I think of all those bulbs that had started to surface which are now buried far below the perfect white surface.

My phone dings.

"I'm struggling. Please tell me this snow does something for the garden."

It's one of my friends from church who is as desperate for spring as I am. Just a few weeks ago we were talking about our hens, how they weren't laying yet, and we were eagerly counting down the days until our baskets were full again. They had just started laying. And now the snow. The snow that's sure to stress them out and slow the egg production again, it seems.

So I pick up my phone and stare at the blank slate scene that feels almost perfectly painted outside of my kitchen window. The empty bird feeder swings in the winds. The garden gate is buried shut. The garden is a stark outline of broken sunflower stalks and brown love-in-a-puff vines drying on the trellis. The greenhouse is covered in white piles and the birdbath is frozen over, with a tiny white hat on the icy mini pond. It happens every year. My husband reminds me of this. He has a photo of every year saved on his phone. The spring snow happens every year and I'm always shocked. I always forget. I can never seem to remember the rhythm of winter ordained to turn into spring.

"The snow feeds nitrogen into the soil," I text my friend as I stand at the window. "The poor man's fertilizer." And Lord, we are poor. Don't I know it. We have enough in our home—enough to pay the bills—but my soul feels poor. My heart feels weary. My body is tired. I am as poor in spirit as they come these days, and the Lord knows I need his work.

The poor man's fertilizer: nitrogen through snow. Nitrogen, which is necessary for all of the things we grow, is depleted quickly from the ground. Tomatoes, greens, corn, peppers, you name it.

They feed on the nitrogen and grow into what we need in mid-summer. The soil needs it, the plants need it, and the snow delivers. In mid-March, when we're hanging the Irish flag and looking for any sign of spring, the snow nurtures the ground. It feeds the soil nutrients for the long days of work ahead. For the season when nitrogen will be sucked from the ground by the hungry greens, the snow replenishes the storehouse. The snow tells us to wait. It tells me to slow down. It pushes *pause*. It tells me: "We're in this together." It covers the shallots and the garlic, the tulips and the crocus, the Star of Holland and the hellebores, and it says: "Not quite yet." Like a mother who leans over her sleeping child at dawn, kisses their forehead and tucks in the blanket to buy just another thirty minutes, so the snow tucks in the earth at springtime. She leans into her velvet winds, her chilled fingers tenderly brushing our praying lips—*just a few more minutes. Keep sleeping. The sun will rise and so will you, but not just yet.*

Lord, help me to remember this when I am ready to jump into the next thing, the next season, the next place you call me to, that I cannot run ahead of you. When I feel you tuck me in instead of setting me loose, remind me that it is not for my suffering but for my gain. When I feel the weight of a winter snow on all of the things I'm dreaming and hoping for, remind me that you can restore in one short painful season more than I can muster up on my own in all my seasons of flourishing. You know what my soul needs. You know where I am depleted. Keep me from the self-sufficiency that wants to raise a fist at your gray and white swirling skies. Teach me to rest and trust you when I want to run and go. Teach me to soak in what you are teaching me when I want to just show off to the world everything I've learned. Teach me to be quiet when I want to shine. Teach me to be poor in spirit so I know your provision when it comes. Teach me to pay attention when you say—*just a few more minutes. Keep sleeping. The sun will rise and so will you, but not just yet.*

## Cultivate

Do not be too eager to start the garden before it is time. While there are a few things that can handle a late season snow (peas, carrots, brassicas), others will wilt and never quite bounce back. Or they'll turn black under the frost, showing the end of their new growth. Have patience. Have patience for the things that demand your faithful stewardship.

Instead, prepare your seeds for planting. Order the last-minute things you may have forgotten. This is a good time to even begin dreaming of how you'll use what you plant. Do you want to try pickles this year? Order the best variety to plant now. You might even find a few local greenhouses will set out some early seedlings or flowers. Bring some of them into your home. Force[3] some tulips and hyacinth from pots at your dining room table as you wait for the world to thaw.

15

# Stuck: The Mud Season

*The love of dirt is among the earliest of passions, as it is the latest. Mud-pies gratify one of our first and best instincts.*

There is an in-between season, between the cold and the blooms, right in the messy middle. The literal messy middle: mud season.

The muck boots are lined up on our back porch, crusted with dirt and chicken manure. The garden paths are thick with cement-like mud and with each walk to and from the greenhouse, I sink deeper into the ground. My sloggers often get stuck and I've lost my footing more than once, only to land with a socked, bootless foot into the slop, leaving the other boot behind.

One year I attempted to plant Bells of Ireland in this kind of weather. (I suppose that's how most gardeners learn—we make a thousand mistakes until we figure out what works.) Planting Bells of Ireland in the spring mud does *not* work. Those poor seeds were swallowed alive in the following days, never to germinate or be seen again. Even the birds knew better than to dig. They waited, unlike me, for the ground to be ready.

At this time of year, when we make the trek up to Vermont to see my in-laws, their road is nearly an amusement park ride. The ruts in the mud are so deep, so unmoving, we remarked last spring that it's basically driver-less steering. The road has determined which way you'll go, like it or not. Mud is a powerful force, the earth coming alive with water—like clay in the Potter's hands—going wherever he commands it. If you've ever experienced a flood, you know it's not just the water that damages everything; it's the inches of mud that seem to cake every surface. Mud stalls everything and forces us to wait, to see where the season takes us. To wash the floors again, check the weather again, and wait one more day for the seasonal signs that we have waited the right amount of time.

The mark of the beginning of spring does not mean it's time to plant everything. As short as the planting season may be in some places, it is also very long. In the same way we quip "life is short!" and encourage one another to seize the day, the reality is that life is also very long. By God's grace and generosity, we might get years and years of redundancy and patience, faithfulness and long-suffering. And so we learn in the spring that there is plenty of time. There is time to wait and pause. Ecclesiastes 3:2 encourages us that there is a time to plant and a time to harvest, and somewhere in between the two, is a time to wait.

## 15 ⁕ Stuck: The Mud Season

Life is very long. I think this day after day, when my attempts at simple living seem more boring than faithful. When we rise in the morning with the same routine—coffee and books and Bible and songs—with breakfast crumbs trailing along the table's edge. A pile of dishes before noon. Corrections, arguments, deep conversations about space, theology, culture, and literature. All these things, wonderful, but my oh my, sometimes they are shockingly long and slow. A road the Potter has formed for me which sometimes feels immoveable—ruts and paths that keep me in one place. The pace doesn't appeal to the soul who longs for immediate results or productivity. It doesn't feed the heart that finds great joy in change or forward motion. Slow seasons require us to do what is right and necessary, not necessarily what we want or demand. If we try and wrangle the sovereignty of God's timing out of his hands, we might only find we're in our socks, ankle deep in mud, wondering where all of our self-driven hard work ended up.

I know this from planting those Bells of Ireland seeds, never to see the work pay off. I sometimes wonder if one of the reasons the Lord tells us to be still and know that he is God, is because one of the prerequisites for knowing his big God-ness is simply being still. It's stopping, *for heaven's sake*. It's letting the churn of mud slow us down enough so we can see who God actually is and where on earth he actually has us. The messy middle. The uncomfortable in-between. The place where redundancy and waiting go hand in hand. There is a time to plant, a time to harvest, and a time to be still and wait for both.

## Cultivate

Take note of places where water gathers heavily around your property. Consider collecting rain, setting out a rain gauge, installing a small water feature, or set in a bird bath. Plant things there that will not get spooked by sogginess. Once again, know your zone and search for plants that can handle the extra moisture when it comes.

And as it goes, take note of the places of your heart that easily get weighed down. Where does your heart tend to slope downhill, a gathering place for the soggy, the bleak, the despair? Teach your heart now the songs to sing when your feet are stuck in the messy middle.

Pray and sing with the words of Psalm 28:6–9:

> Blessed be the LORD!
> > For he has heard the voice of my pleas for mercy.
>
> The LORD is my strength and my shield;
> > in him my heart trusts, and I am helped;
>
> my heart exults,
> > and with my song I give thanks to him.
>
> The LORD is the strength of his people;
> > he is the saving refuge of his anointed.
>
> Oh, save your people and bless your heritage!
> > Be their shepherd and carry them forever.

Carry me, O Lord, when my feet cannot carry me any further.
When the slopes of my heart all drain inward,
and I find myself in places

## 15 ❧ Stuck: The Mud Season

where my joy feels soggy, like an old sponge
that was never wrung out.
Help me, O Lord, when the things I have carried
seem old, boring, redundant.
Have mercy on my too-easily entertained and distracted heart.
Carry me on your shoulders as a lamb
who is stuck out in the pasture
and needs to come home.

Hear my bleating cries for mercy,
give me faith to follow your heritage,
keep me safe in your refuge,
be my strength.

## 16

# The Prep Season

*Oh, Adam was a gardener, and God who made him sees*
*That half a proper gardener's work is done upon his knees*

*It's the first* warm day of March which means it's the first time it feels somewhat close to gardening season where I live. I have left most of the clean-up to the spring for one main reason: it's easier. There are other reasons, of course, but in the spring the dried-out woody stalks simply pull straight out of the soil. This too is a grace because I spent some blood, sweat, and tears last autumn trying to pull these out without losing half of my soil beds. Some things are simply better left to care for after winter. And so it's March, mind you, barely coming off of the last snow, and I am pulling up woody stems and raking the rotted remains of what was left behind.

The old gourd vines are twisted brown around the trellis, and they easily snap right off as I pull against them. I'm mostly spending this time talking to myself about what I should have done last

## 16 ※ The Prep Season

year, what I should have planted elsewhere or not all (especially as I pull the perennial tansy from one of the vegetable beds.) This year we have determined to be more vigorous against the volunteers. These are the fruits and vegetables that happily reseed themselves. Each year, hundreds of tomato volunteers pop up in the beds. The birds fill the garden with the sunflower seeds that fell from their beaks, and now they pop up like happy toddlers in the early morning. The perennials return. The mint sprawls. The amaranth shows up unexpectedly. Scallions I must have forgotten poke their tiny green heads from the end of the bed. The volunteers are eager and work hard. Several summers ago, the garden nearly broke me. It was a year when we underestimated our schedule, overestimated our energy, and did not plan for a newly-expanded garden as we should have. I was not relentless about the weeds and even less interested in pulling what I considered to be healthy volunteers. And I paid for it. I paid for it in sunflowers that grew through my cabbage and celery beds. Tomatoes that took over my squash. Black-eyed Susans that pushed their beefy leaves deep and wide across my pepper patch.

And then there were the weeds.

Lord, have mercy, the weeds.

This is not the last time you will read about weeds, blood, and sweat in this humble book. I'm here to tell you that weeds will show up in every season of gardening. I find it interesting that worldly philosophers will write about gardens and the nasty work of weeding, but they simply fail to see how this very work is one of the common graces of nature. God is teaching us through his creation if only we are be humble enough to learn.

And in one year of lazy weeding, exhausted vision, and too much garden for our schedule, the weeds took over. The volunteers dominated. The rudbeckia jumped into new beds and started all over again for round two in August. As wildly beautiful as it was, I cried when I couldn't even walk the pathways for how much work there was to be done. So don't be fooled—you will work for your garden one way or another. Do the hard work now or do the hard work then, but hard work will be required of you. So now is the prep season. Now is when I steel my mind to do the work when the time comes. Now is when I pull at any green leaf in the beds, even when I know they're technically not "weeds."

If I'm being honest, I struggle to let things go. I lean heavily toward nostalgia, still holding on to that paper ornament my (now fourteen-year-old) daughter gave me when she was four. I have a box of drawings and notes and cards from my children that I can't seem to part with. Just recently, I found a box tucked in my closet with some of my son's keepsakes. It was full of clothes, cute little boy flannels and baby Irish caps, hand-knit sweaters and bright yellow pants with snails on them. It took a great amount of reality-checking for me to admit that he won't want these anymore. A daughter—maybe she would enjoy some clothes from her baby years. But a son? In the event he gets married someday and has children of his own, I know right now I am risking the relationship with my future daughter-in-law if I were to hand her a box of his baby clothes. These are things I need to part with now, while he's still five and missing a tooth, not when he's twenty-five and his poor wife looks at me as if to say: "Thanks, now I have to get rid of these since you didn't have the heart to do it back then."

We cling to memories, experiences, relationships, emotional highs, successes; these things which are true parts of our stories risk becoming the things we build our lives around. We try to plant new seasons of life around last season's woody and dry flower remains. We try to make room for things we've held on to year after year, volunteer growth that we weren't willing to move, and now it sticks around, claiming territory in our hearts. Instead of looking at each season of our life, asking the Lord what he wants to remove and make new, we become like the Israelites, planting Egypt in our hearts again and again. We look like Lot's wife, looking back at what we had instead of running toward what we need. We become like the disciples who keep asking the wrong questions instead of seeing Jesus right in front of them. We're doomed to repeat what we don't want to repeat when we fool ourselves into thinking we don't need to be made completely new. We don't need a good night's sleep; we need death and resurrection.

We have to let things die that are already dead. A strange conundrum for sure. Yet in the garden, when I'm pulling the stems of the old peppers or removing the kale I didn't want in that bed, I'm finishing the work of putting to death that which has already produced death. We have to be diligent about this work in our own hearts.

That old relationship that only feeds bitterness or longing within you? Time to let it go.

That success in your early twenties that was at least fifteen years ago now? Time to move on.

That job, title, role that became your entire identity but was suddenly removed with a pink slip, company change, or someone else's promotion? Time to remove what was and start planning for what will be.

That crushed dream, lost hope, imagined life plan that never came to fruition? Grieve. Take a deep breath. And then clear the beds. It's time for something new.

We don't hang our hopes on last year's garden. We don't plan our tables on last year's harvest. We don't set our hearts on the browned, dried out stems of last season's beauty. We put it all on Christ, knowing that he is making all things new, doing what only he can do.

So get to work. Prep your garden. New things are coming, and we are going to be ready for them.

## Cultivate

If you are new to gardening, start planning where you will plant. Prepare the beds. Till the soil. Lay down cardboard to start killing the grass. Mark out your plots. Build the raised beds. If this isn't your first year, get to work now on weeding and removing what remains from last year. If a perennial needs to go, remove it now. If a volunteer shows up, assess if this is where you want it. If not, pull it or move it somewhere else. Remove the dry stalks, old vines, dead leaves, and make room for the new season.

Lord, I'm standing at the edge of the new season but it's hard to let go of what was. I know you want to do new things in me, but my heart is attached to what remains of who I used to be. Help me to let go.

There are places I used to feel life, but they are empty now. Bring new life to me.

There are places I used to see beauty, but they are ugly now. Restore to me the joy of your salvation.

There are places I used to bring in a harvest that are now ____. Help me to see hope in the barrenness.

There are places I used to celebrate and now they're silent. Help me to see how you make all things new.

Keep me from wrapping my heart around empty places, barren ground, frozen earth, and shells of remembrance. Keep me from making a home here in memory and nostalgia only. Help me to remember how to entrust you with this fallow ground.

## 17

# Watch the Birds

*The robins were singing vespers in the high tree-tops,*
*filling the golden air with their jubilant voices.*

*T*he *birds started* singing at 4:39 a.m. today. I cracked one eye open to see if I was hearing things; if a songbird had decided she would sing us all to sleep. The sky was a deep sapphire blue, the first sign that the sun is coming soon. She sang and twittered her song of morning on the lilac outside of our bedroom window.

Some scientists suggest that one of the reasons birds sing so early in the morning is to let their other feathered friends know that they survived the night.[4]

"I made it," she'll sing, eyes pointed at the edge of dawn. "I'm still here!"

This feels similar to what we do with our country neighbors after the first big thaw. Usually someone will step out in front of their porch, picking up sticks or just surveying what is happening outside post-winter. We'll wave and one of us says something like

"You made it through another winter!" Our other neighbor will suddenly be out on his Gator cart again, waving to us across the field, another sign to say "We're still here!"

By the end of winter, I fully restock our bird feeders. One hangs just outside the kitchen window, the place where the hollyhock and lily trees will stand seven-feet tall by summertime but are now dormant and still underground. We look daily for the first red cardinal. His appearance marks the beginning of spring for me. Well, his appearance and the cluster of red-breasted robins that gather over the lower field to peck at whatever worms have started surfacing. These are signs that the winter is ending. Suddenly the birds are out making nests, collecting seeds, singing at dawn, flitting from the birdbath and along the top of the garden fences. The goldfinches hop around happily and the black-capped chickadees sing their "chicka-dee-dee-dee" song from the still bare bushes. They're all singing survivor songs. Winter did not win. Winter is not the end. We're watching them and paying attention to the rhythms they know, down to their DNA.[5]

I can pace my seed planting by how haphazardly the house sparrow is building a nest inside of the barn siding. Every year they return to the same barn siding that has split away from under the awning, a good twelve feet above our heads. Every year they sing and scream in panic: "The babies are coming! Winter is over!" and we watch as they dive in and out, each day, in a hurry. These anxious parents are my sign that I should get the garden ready. One afternoon of laying out fresh compost will bring all of the spring birds to feast and they'll wash in the birdbath filled with thawed snow.

All of this reminds me I should check my calendar again for when the last frost is due, and double check all of my seeds to see if there are any I've forgotten. (Which I always do! This year I completely neglected to buy any green beans of any kind, much to the disappointment of my daughter.) When the birds start moving around the garden, I know it's time to plant the peas, the spinach, and the other seeds that love the cold. The birds give hints—the ground is ready, the chicks are coming, spring is humming her song at the edge of dawn—we can start singing along.

There are songs that rise up in me at dawn, during my day-to-day chores, or when I need to sing in the face of fear or suffering. *Great Is Thy Faithfulness* is one of those. *As The Deer* often hums to the surface. For me, singing raises some small weapon against the battering of this world. To sing, to worship, to praise—it is a kind of protest against despair, cynicism, and shadows. The song that comes out from me isn't one I usually choose; it is usually one that was impressed so deeply into my memory and experience that it has become a part of who I am. When the songbirds sing the same songs, I know the feeling. When we sing them at church, I am reminded that these are the songs we return to again and again. These are the songs we've been singing for years, lifetimes even, songs that remind us of where to go, what to believe, where to keep our eyes when the winter feels long.

Watch the birds, in so many ways, because they teach us about what it means to depend on the songs within us and the predictability of the seasons around us, set in place by our Father who has not lost track of us yet.

## Cultivate

"Look at the birds of the air: they neither sow nor reap nor gather into barns, and yet your heavenly Father feeds them. Are you not of more value than they?" (Matthew 6:26)

Stock the bird feeders. Consider the birds of the air. Pay attention to their patterns. There are different kinds of birdseed, so when you're looking, get what best serves the birds that are native to your area. Fill feeders for the songbirds, the colorful birds, and indulge in your curiosity by learning their breeds, their songs. In addition to ordinary old feeders, you can set out hummingbird feeders, oriole feeders, peanut butter feeders, and so on. The joy of watching the birds come back will be enough to make you want to grab some binoculars and an Audubon book.

Let this old hymn soar in your heart as you go about your days:

This is my Father's world:
The birds their carols raise,
The morning light, the lily white,
Declare their Maker's praise.
This is my Father's world:
He shines in all that's fair;
In the rustling grass I hear Him pass,
He speaks to me everywhere.[6]

# 18

# Planting and Tending Seeds and the Starts

*The man who undertakes a garden is relentlessly pursued. ...
He has planted a seed that will keep him awake nights;
drive rest from his bones, and sleep from his pillow.*

*Everyone loves* a garden in bloom. But not everyone loves when I start rattling off my list of what to do in February, March, April, and May. We all like to think that beautiful things simply appear. You have a lucky blend of spices in the meal. You cooked the steak just perfectly by accident. They just had good chemistry and that's why their marriage lasted. She just happened to be good at quilting and that's why she can make those bedspreads so easily.

The hard truth is—none of that is real. If you want to have a good meal, perfect steak, a marriage that endures, heirloom quilts, and a basket full of flowers, herbs, and vegetables, you must put in the work.

So let's talk shop.

I start about ninety percent of our seeds every year. The other ten percent is what fails so I go out to a local greenhouse and buy their very healthy versions of what I managed to kill. But January dreaming begets February charting, and inventorying begets the massive countdown calendar and seed starting. I used to start all of my seeds in those plastic cell trays you can buy at any big box store. They'll usually start appearing around March or April. While they're relatively affordable, they also don't have a very long shelf life. You can invest in higher quality trays which will last season to season, but if it is not something you're too worried about, the Walmart versions are just fine. Just this past season I've started soil-blocking instead of using cell trays. I'm not nearly adept enough at it yet to give any advice here, but it seems my garden loved the method.

All that to say, you need something to start your seeds in. Purchasing good quality seed-starting soil will help significantly. I would make sure that this is something you are willing to invest in. Don't use potting soil. Don't use topsoil. Get some quality sifted seed-starting mix, preferably organic if you can, and use that. I buy ours in bulk, and the poor FedEx man has to shoulder the burden to my back porch in the dead of winter while I hide in my kitchen, hoping he doesn't see me. But I digress.

Take some time, one slow late winter or early spring day, to check the planting recommendations for all your seeds. Figure out when the last frost is and count backwards. Have a plan for when you're going to plant each seed packet. The worst thing you could do for your garden is to assume everything gets planted the same week. It's simply not true. I stagger my planting beginning at week twelve of the countdown, starting new seeds every two weeks until I can plant seeds directly in the ground. Some vegetables or flowers really do not like to be transplanted. Take note of those things. Some really don't like to be crowded, and some prefer a crowd of friends to grow up with. Note this as well.

All this to say—do the grueling, tedious, and somewhat boring work of learning about everything you're starting, planting, and growing. When you learn something like tomatoes don't like to be crowded, you'll be thankful you remember that when you're transferring those plants to your beds.

The details matter. The work matters. The soil, the schedule, the timing, the watering, the lighting, the temperatures, it all does actually matter. We are not Jack growing a beanstalk. There are no magic beans, only diligent hands.

Almost twenty years ago, I managed to make a series of catastrophic mistakes that really blew my life up. I mean, I made a significant mess of things. After a few years of wandering and trying out the local pig slop, by the grace of God, I came home. Some well-meaning (or perhaps not) church person stopped me once to tell me that while I was certainly welcome back home, I shouldn't expect to receive my status back as a well-loved child of God. I had squandered my inheritance. I was now living the Plan B for my life, which God would still bless but not nearly as much had I stayed faithful the whole time. Even as I write this, I realize that was probably not well-intentioned. It's quite sinister to even type out.

Because if there's one thing I have learned about following God up to this point in my life, it is that God is not operating in plan A, plan B, plan M, or plan 2.0. He has *a plan*, a very detailed, specific timeline for us. He sees and knows all of the details and is able to sovereignly work all things together for our good and his glory. He is aware of what will grow us, what will make us strong, what soil we need, what rains we will soak up. Nothing is outside of his care and attention. He is not a sky genie hoping that we ask for the right thing. He is joyfully arranging all of the details.

So, perhaps in this season, in our care and tending to the fragile things of the garden, this is how we image our Father. We follow him around as eager children, watching as his hands do the busy work and tend to his creation, and we learn about how to do that just like him in the dirt of creation itself.

## Cultivate

Work on a sowing calendar. If you're going to start your own seeds, start planning now. Mark the last frost and count backwards. Decide which seed trays you'll use or if you'll try a different method. Plan for the light you'll need, make sure the seedlings have a warm place, and protect them from things like curious cats and children, harsh winds and cold, and other pests. Research best methods for sowing each variety, note the ones that need plenty of start time

*Spring*

before the planting season and the ones that are best sown directly into the ground, and be ready to take as many notes as you can. This is usually the time of year I start my garden journal so that I can remember what I'm doing each week as I look back. The details are the work these days; don't miss them.

19

# Potting Up, Hardening Off, and Withstanding Winds

*And after you have suffered a little while, the God of all grace,*
*who has called you to his eternal glory in Christ,*
*will himself restore, confirm, strengthen, and establish you.*

*I talk to my seedlings*, further locking in my status as that "weird garden lady." But all spring long, when I check on them, I am encouraging them, asking them how they're doing, chiding the ones who seem to be rebelling, and gently encouraging the ones who really do struggle. It's my job to know them. It's my job to know what is where and what they need. It is the gardener's job to be intimately acquainted with each tiny detail that will help them survive. Every year, I eventually get to the point where it is thrive, survive, or die and that's about all of the love they get from me in late August. But in April? May? I am a kinder mother, imaging my own Father who teaches me what it means to pay attention to the details of the small growing things. The soil temperature, humidity, air temperature, how I water, spacing: it all matters.

If you are growing tomatoes, celery, peppers, brassicas, or anything else that is rapidly outgrowing your initial seed trays, you'll want to plan to pot up. Potting up is when you move the smaller seedlings, or maybe even separate out a cluster of seedlings into larger pots, soil blocks, or trays with larger cells. This happens after the seedling has shown its true leaves. Most seedlings emerge with the same small green sprouts, but don't be fooled—those are not the true leaves. These are called cotyledons, and they all look very similar from plant to plant. After a few days or even weeks, the true leaves eventually unfold, thus revealing the true heritage of the plant. Once the seedling gets too big for the space, usually sometime around six to eight weeks after you started it, it's ready to be rehomed to a larger space. This is a tender and slow work, though in reality, these baby seedlings can take a hardy root shake and separation from their siblings who grew up with them. Most of them will do just fine if you tenderly separate them and place them in new soil on their own. This also prevents them from getting root bound, which no plant enjoys. Because the reality is there's only so much soil. If you have ever set a seed tray inside of a water tray, you know that the network of roots can become an almost alien-like web, filling the space below the seedlings almost as quickly as the seedlings fill the space above. The more room you can give roots, the better.

It's a tedious process. I've spent many hours over the spring afternoons carefully moving celery seedlings from one massive, multi-sown tray to single soil blocks. It almost feels pointless. In fact, last year I wasn't convinced it was worth the extra work and just let them grow bigger in the multi-sown tray. To test my theory, I planted about ten in single soil blocks. The rest crowded one another and grew, waiting for the planting season.

By the time I got them into the ground, the ones I had taken the time to move to single soil blocks were sturdy and ready to be hardened off. They survived a couple cold nights, and eventually grew into large celery stalks, bringing in a robust harvest mid-summer. However, the ones I didn't take the time to pot up suffered to the point of death. Only one or two actually made it (out of forty or so), and they were small, weak, and meager. The takeaway? The hard, tedious work is worth it. Of course, we all know this but every now and then a gardener likes to try her luck.

> In addition, wind blowing on a small seedling or newly emerged spring plant helps the plant create a stronger stem. Each time a plant is pushed by the wind, it releases a hormone called an auxin that stimulates the growth of supporting cells. Research has shown that this is actually beneficial to the plant, and that plants that begin growth in the absence of wind tend fall over or break more easily than those grown in the presence of some wind. Anyone who has ever started garden plants from seeds has probably experienced this. The best way to avoid wind damage to seedlings is to place them outside for short periods of time each day, to "harden off" the plants from the effects of the wind and direct sunlight.[7]

*Spring*

When the winter days move into spring, that springtime lion begins his roar. With each spring rain that splashes against my kitchen windows, I breathe a small sigh of relief and remind myself: "This could have been snow." As our overnight temperatures stop dropping below thirty-two degrees, I slowly begin the process of moving the trays out of our grow room and into the cold frame. If the days warm up but the nights stay cold, I still bring the trays out onto the back steps to get their own sunshine and wind. It feels a bit like introducing little children to the big world. The reality of garden life is just beginning, and I'm entrusting their small, brand new stalks to the brutality of a harsh world. The spring world is seventy degrees one minute and forty the next. As Charles Dickens famously wrote in *Great Expectations:* "It was one of those March days when the sun shines hot and the wind blows cold: when it is summer in the light, and winter in the shade." All of the winds feel bold in the spring, as though winter is giving one last send-off. The newly budding tree branches thrash and some fall to the ground, covering our yard with sticks for the kids to pickup as their next Saturday chore. For the seedlings that don't require extra care and consolation, those trays will line the path leading to the cold frame door. The winds will whip along their surface, flipping the small leaves and bending them sideways. In a moment of worry, I might be tempted to think that this wind is too much; that it will break them.

I think this of my children sometimes. And of friends and church family—that when the winds blow, it could be too harsh

## 19 ⁕ Potting Up, Hardening Off, and Withstanding Winds

for their young faith, young hearts, and new growth. Could it be that God has put within us something that causes our roots to anchor more deeply into the secure foundation of Christ when the winds blow? We are like trees, planted by streams of living water, not blown this way and that way, but rooted deeply in the ground.

Here is what I know to be true: in his most beautiful, sovereign grace, the Lord provided a way through the suffering, not around it. In that auxin that he gave those plants, they learn how to stand more firm, how to stand more sure. This process is called hardening off and it certainly is a fitting term. These plants, after having done everything to stand firm, stand. After a season of nurturing and tender care and protection, the only way they survive is to face the hardships and suffering head-on. When the days are windless, I will walk along the trays and run my hands over the greens. I will brush the tops of the tomatoes, snapdragons, peppers—this small gesture—a reminder that I am near and it is time to grow.

Of course, I've had my share of hardening-off failures. The mice that ate months worth of work of flowers and herbs when I neglected to pick the trays up off the ground overnight. The greenhouse full of sensitive seedlings that I neglected to cover on a particularly bitterly cold night. The ones I forgot to water. The day I forgot to open the door of the greenhouse and the internal temperatures soared over one hundred degrees, cooking all of the seedlings inside. It only takes a few summers of working in a garden to realize that failure is both immanent and unavoidable. No matter how much you know and how much you plan, you can't foresee the day that the cats knock the tray of baby pepper plants off of the growing shelves. Or the failure of onions, even though they looked healthy and fine last week. Or the Japanese Beetles that decide to feast on your roses and dahlias. You can learn, no doubt, but you can't prepare for everything. This is why we harden them off. They need within them the thing that will fight to survive, fight to send the roots deeper, fight to produce flowers, fruit, and life.

And so as the snow turns to rain, and the fields fade into that subtle, goldish-green spring, we prepare ourselves for the days ahead. The days of work, of joy, of deeper roots, of unpredictable storms, of disheartening failures, and the winds that will only make us more certain in the place where we stand.

This is the work that pays off in springtime. One year, I felt lazy and attempted to plant my onion seedlings straight in the ground without hardening them off, and they all died. It was a high price to pay for a shortcut. I think humans need this process too. Think about how we slowly adjust to the outdoors after winter. We attempt shorts on the first fifty-degree day and regret it once the snow decides to fly in the late afternoon. We try to wear sweaters and scarves in September only to find our faces melting off when it is still ninety-five degrees. We all need the space for adjustment; give your seedlings the same grace. It is in the hardening off process that they learn to stand tall in the wind, their roots growing stronger day by day.

The analogies I could draw for you in these things alone could take hours. I just keep thinking, "Consider the lilies of the field ..."

## 19 ❦ Potting Up, Hardening Off, and Withstanding Winds

Except, in this case: consider the celery and tomatoes that the gardener faithfully tended. If they can grow and survive and be cared for by tender, acute hands, won't he do the same for us? If I can remember to give my roots space and bring them into healthy soil for optimal growth, won't he also care for my roots, encouraging me toward good soil, and healthy places to stretch my soul into the deepest layers of grace? If I, a sometimes lazy gardener, can manage to take the time to tediously pot up hundreds of garden seedlings so that they'll thrive in the garden, don't you think our Father pays attention to what is best for our growth? The glory of the gardener is when the garden grows! What kind of fruit would we be if we failed for lack of care? His joy is that we delight in all he does to help us grow. If I can remember that hardening off is what is best for my seedlings because I want them to grow and not wilt, then don't you think it is possible our faithful Father, who walks the garden at the cool of the day, knows exactly what our roots need to grow? He is not lazy. He is not weary of tedium. We are not toys he experiments on to see what happens. He loves us. And so we entrust our souls to his tender, precise care.

### Cultivate

If you are growing your own seeds, pay attention to when it's time to pot up and harden off your seedlings. Have a plan for what pots you'll use. Ideally, they're a couple of inches bigger than what they're already growing in. If the weather is starting to be more mild and days are warmer, start to bring your seedlings out during the day in a safe place to harden them off. A back porch, front step, back deck, open fire escape landing—give them fresh air and sunlight. If you're not doing your own seedlings, start to pay attention to when local greenhouses are opening up. If it's close to potting up and hardening off season, it's likely your local farmers are almost ready to open their doors.

20

# The Return of Life

*Spring mornings are tangible proof that God is still pursuing us with his mercy.*

*It's as though* I fell asleep one winter's night, and in a blink, the entire garden returned to life. The voracious green of field and forest came alive through one rolling, midnight thunderstorm. One spring rain brought on the leaves. Those seeds I planted weeks ago, in such a determined hope have now not only germinated but are ready to be harvested. The demand of the garden has started, taking its shape in the small heart-shaped form of baby spinach leaves. All season I wait for that first harvest; it's sweeter than almost any other harvest of the year. Both literally and figuratively. The cold has sweetened the leaves of the spinach and if I cut them early enough in the morning, I'll still be able to retain the sugar in the leaves. But it's also sweeter because I am a person who forgets. I forget that the seeds I plant will actually grow. I forget what a joy it is to fill an entire basket and bring it indoors. How is it possible to forget such a consistent and predictable thing?

I leak, I suppose. Winter creates cracks in me that I don't find until I try to fill myself up again. The faith and confidence I carried so fully into the fall snuck out the door when I wasn't paying attention. My faith feels small and tired. I feel as cold as the soil I planted those pea seeds in just weeks ago. Yet somehow any sign of life in me feels sweeter than I anticipated it would.

Our old farmhouse I grew to loathe by the end of March is now a bustling garden house. The dreaded field that called for my sweat and vision is now covered with mulch and clean edges. The frost-covered winter mornings are now filled with songs of praise from the robins and chickadees. The frogs sing in the ponds at night. If his mercies are new every morning, then spring is one long morning for creation. It is pure mercy that life has returned. It is mercy that the cold things become the sweetest things. It's a mercy that I can plant with ice still on the birdbath and reap when the dew is fresh.

It is truly God's mercy that he continues to give us this earth to tend, care for, and cultivate. It is a mercy to hold my kids in my arms every morning. It is mercy to turn my head into my husband's shoulder when he hugs me. It is mercy that allows me to simply live and wait with creation for full redemption and it is mercy to see hints of it in the shadowed and cold places of this earth.

The radishes have grown, the lettuce is lush, and the peas are just an inch above ground, already looking for a place to climb. As their small tendrils uncurl and reach, I nudge them closer to the fence edge. Mercy is the gentle hand that guides in the way we should go. Mercy is the work of the Gardener who knows where he planted us, why, when, and then directs our winter-weary hands toward the places we can lean.

The fences, the walls, the trellis, the house, the church, and the family.

If peas, spinach, and lettuce are not left alone, but are rather nurtured and sweetened in the ground by God, then neither are we left to languish. What mercy, indeed.

## Cultivate

This world is a battered and tired place, longing for redemption. We ache along with it and crane our necks for hopeful signs of redemptive spring. However, in our creatureliness, we tend to look in the wrong places—the news cycles, election seasons, money, material possessions—when my soul encounters the goodness of God in someone else, I often find something inside me, stirring to life again. When we give mercy to one another—when we continue to pour out kindness and gospel love to each other instead of stinging words, bitterness, or hatred—the ground begins to rumble a little with the song of redemption. So, as spring returns to the soil, perhaps we should ask ourselves how we can usher in the goodness and kindness of God wherever we go in this cold world. Where can you show mercy?

## 21

# The Thinning Season

*There is nothing wasted in the garden.*

*The thinning season* always brings me to tears. Maybe because I have felt the thinning season myself; the uprooting that occurs and feels so close to my own roots. I sometimes wonder if the life will get pulled out of me too. I know what it feels like to work hard at something and have it disappear before my eyes. I know what it is like to pour my heart and energy and blood into something, only to see the Lord pull it away from me just as I thought it was going to thrive. It takes the breath from my lungs. It makes my heart wilt and my throat tighten.

So, as we near planting season and the soil blocks are bursting with healthy cabbage and peppers and tomatoes, zinnias and statice and stock, it is time for me to thin them. There are choices of course—replant the seedling into a new cell, toss the seedling into the compost, toss the seedling into the dirt beneath my feet, or leave them alone and let them all suffer. See, most plants need space. They need their own root space, a healthy circumference away from the other plants. Most of them won't do well if they're crowded. Yes, even plants have a personal space bubble. For the best chance of the healthiest plant with the least amount of disease, the thinning season must take place.

Seedling by seedling, I remove the weaker ones until the healthiest remain. This always hurts. Since day one, I have watched these seeds unfold and reach toward the light. Since day one, I have watered them, cared for them, believed in them, knowing full well that not all of them would reach maturity. No matter how healthy they are, some of them just won't make it to the end. There is no heavenly analogy that brings me comfort here. The reality is that some things that look healthy just don't make it. Healthy faiths. Healthy bodies. Healthy dreams. Some of them just don't make it, and there isn't always a clear reason why. At least not to the seedling.

But I know. I know what I'm doing.

Some get moved to a fresh pot of soil.

Some get moved to a neighboring cell where another seed never germinated.

Some get thrown into the compost and in six months, I'll find they grew despite the trauma.

Some get thrown onto the ground at my feet, and they'll take over the greenhouse while I sleep.

And some die. They wither away without place or purpose.

*Spring*

The thinning season is a sad season, but not without reason. I am not mindlessly or carelessly doing this work. I am not destructive. It is a slow and careful work. A gentle work.

Maybe this is why it moves me so deeply. In the thinning seasons of my own life, I can almost feel the breath of the Gardener on my face. He pulls gently at what must be moved. He relocates that which I hoped would stay. He tosses those things which do not help. He pulls gently at tender root systems, untangling them from what will remain. He is slow. Gentle. Patient. Careful. This is the work he does through his word: removing, dividing, and piercing to the roots. This is the work of the Spirit, who does the sanctifying work of knowing what belongs, where it belongs, when it stays, and when it's time to pull it away before it takes full root.

Apply this where you will, but it no doubt shows up in different ways. I think of the friends who have had their dreams pulled away overnight. Jobs that suddenly don't pan out. Relationships that ended abruptly. Or even more pointedly, a sharp rebuke from a friend about a blind spot. An argument with my husband that addresses where I've been selfish. A moment with a child where I realize I've been focused on myself. The "no" when all I wanted was a "yes."

Places where I thought there was life, but it was about to be thinned.

This is the life we live—watching as the Lord continues his work among his people, within his church, within our stories. He is never distracted, never late to the process and, as hard as we try

## 21 ※ The Thinning Season

to understand, we are under the mercy of the Gardener who knows all that we do not.

> The thinning work is near, I know
> I feel his breath against the soil
> I hear his humming as he uproots
> the tender, green, thriving shoots
> I thought they were a part of me
> but the Gardener sees what I can't see
> and so he pulls what I held dear
> the gaping dirt of what I feared
> I hear again his gentle song
> as he thins what does not belong

### Cultivate

Take an inventory of your life—where you spend your time, money, energy, and attention. Write down every place you have invested a part of your life and heart. Now, look at it and pray, asking, *Where might the Lord want to thin me? Where can I participate in the thinning?* If there are practical ways to surrender and open your hands to things the Lord is asking you to let go of, write them down, pray, and trust that the thinning work is for your good and his glory. This work might affect commitments, your belongings, weaknesses that you chalk up to "personality traits," relationships, finances, and so many other places where we crowd our lives and world with things that are not intended to live with us forever.

*Spring*

If you are growing seedlings, this might be the season you narrow the cells down to one seedling. If you aren't starting seeds indoors, perhaps this is a chance to look around your heart and home as you prepare for the spring. What do you need to let go of?

## 22

# The Resurrection Season

*Practice resurrection.*

*Every year,* I doubt it. Every year I think, there is no way that tree is still alive. There is no way the peonies will return. There is no way that rose bush will return.

And yet, I am always proved wrong. The lilac pushes out fresh, green growth. The peonies' red stems push out of the dark earth. The roses unfold their leaves and buds sit heavy on their stems. It happens every year. The world shouts with resurrection glory.

*You thought we were dead forever?* The leaves sing for joy and the trees clap their hands.

*You thought we had wasted away?* The tulip bulbs push up from the muddy earth.

*You thought we were forgotten?* The garlic stems push up green and white from the ice-sodden ground.

Lord, why do I forget? You have written your plan for making all things new right onto the cellular design of every living thing in creation. You have been shouting this to us every spring, when we see the earth made new. When we see dead things come to life. Your creation has been waiting to celebrate. Your creation groans with expectation. *Can't you see?*

*He will make all things new.*
*He will do it again.*

## Cultivate

Look up what time the sun rises tomorrow. Set your alarm so you can wake up to see the sunrise and spend time outside, reading John 20. Read the whole chapter out loud as the sun rises. Remember what it must have been like for Mary in the garden to meet Jesus in the cool of the day. Remember his resurrection.

## 23

# The Stormy Season

*For land that has drunk the rain that often falls on it, and produces a crop useful to those for whose sake it is cultivated, receives a blessing from God.*

*The spring storm* starts on the horizon just behind the trees, like a foggy hedgerow of gray. The air is heavy and thick, and we're working in the garden and the field, sweat not dropping but more accumulating on my forehead, my back, and even the inside of my wrists has gathered moisture. They say the heat wouldn't be so bad if it wasn't for the humidity. But it's also May. The heat doesn't usually swallow us whole like this in May.

What sounds like a low rumble, pushes through the air. Was it a passing truck? No, I know what a spring storm looks like as it gathers. She picks up her skirts in a very royal form, as if to parade her imminent arrival. The leaves turn over and bow. The grass waves in procession. The first few breezes pierce the thick air, and we know

*Spring*

it's time to gather the tools, put away the seedlings, and call the children. It's about to storm.

I remember living in Texas and the way the spring and summer storms could easily halt an afternoon. A storm wasn't just something you watched from the kitchen windows; it was something that could shatter them. The storms halt life here too but we open the windows a bit, the dogs run for cover under the beds, and someone says something about how "it'll pass."

Within minutes of collecting our things and running indoors, the sun has disappeared and the whole landscape is under a shadow. I watch from the kitchen window as the garden seems to drink the rain. All the small seedlings reach to the sky signaling another day of provision. Another day of afternoon rain. *Lord,* I nearly gasp, *what a gift.*

*Why do I strain and strive for the things you promise to provide? Why do I drop my own sweat on the dust and think you will not also return water to the wells?*

I know Jesus lived through storms when he walked this earth. I wonder if he laughed when it thundered, hearing the echoes of his own voice ripple across the sky. As the rain pours, I think of Isaiah's call: "Come, everyone who thirsts, come to the waters" (55:1).

*Come, let us open our hands and let the rain wash us again. Let's stop trying to be self-sufficient when the Lord knows we need the skies to break open.*

And then there's the night storm. The one that shows up in the pitch black, rumbling in the distance like a train we cannot

## 23 ✤ *The Stormy Season*

see but know is chugging this way. The lightning fills the sky only long enough for us to wonder if what we see is really there and that yes indeed, the barn is still standing. The rain covers the hot macadam roads and wisps of steam begin to rise across the lanes of headlights. Worms and frogs slither out from their resting places and cover the asphalt. The dogs once again take their place under the bed, shaking and tucking their tails. And we sleep. I follow my Master in this rest, knowing the storms of earth will rage but I can rest. There may be nights of weeping, but tonight is not that night. The storm, without threat or fear, surrounds us in its steady warm fountain. The Lord has found us again—here in the shadowed places, he has not forgotten us.

"But he was in the stern, asleep on the cushion" (Mark 4:38).

While the disciples were fearing for their lives, Jesus was asleep on a pillow. I know that God never sleeps (Psalm 121:3), but Jesus, the man, did. And there's something to be said here—that while the disciples were afraid they would die—Jesus was comfortably snoozing. He didn't sleep on a bare surface to prove he didn't need comfort. He didn't need to be an insomniac to prove his sovereignty. He rested too. Even in the storm. Even in the chaos. Even in the midst of people screaming in panic, he rested his head on a pillow and slept. This is a gift to be understood. The ship isn't going down; Jesus is comfortable, still here, resting on the pillow.

I think of the disciples on that boat with Jesus. That wild storm whipping around their sails and their desperate cries against the howling winds. The tossing aside, this way and that, flipping men off their feet and their master, asleep in the stern on a pillow (Mark 4:35–41). It's not Jesus who needs proving. It's us. This work that the storms and rains and winds bring either makes us think the ship is going down or it has us looking for Jesus.

The storms will roll through, and we can still trust him. Even as we follow him in our sleep.

## Cultivate

Pray this prayer as you face the storms of this season, whether those be thunderheads or invisible to everyone else but you:

Lord, when the storms gather on the horizon, teach me to look for you. Help me to see you, not panicking or throwing anchors overboard. Help me to entrust my soul to you when the clouds gather. You who command the wind and the waves. You who designed the white caps and the lightning. You who shroud yourself in the mystery of thunder (Nahum 1:3)—teach me to seek you first before I seek my own wellbeing, for in you I am well.

Lord, you are my refuge from the storm and rain (Isaiah 4:6). Help me to remember that all I must do is run to you.

Lord, you rule the raging of the sea (Psalm 89:9). Please calm the raging in my heart. Lord, on these tempest-tossed days, help me to trust that your faithfulness is not at stake. Bring me to my desired haven in You (Psalm 107:23–30).

Lord, remind me that you bring the rain, more abundantly and sufficient than the sweat of my brow. Fill these fields in your faithfulness (Zechariah 10:1).

## 23 · *The Stormy Season*

Father, you alone make the rain, the soil, the seeds, the growth, the vegetables, the flowers, the fruit, the leaves, the sun, the clouds, the seasons, and you have set all of these within your boundaries. Help me see how you have safely kept me within your hands as well (John 10:28–30).

## 24

# The War of the Weeds, *Part One*

*Never delay weeding.*

*It's another warm* spring day, the kind that invites us outdoors as soon as we're able. Even breakfast is put on hold as muck boots are pulled up over our work jeans and one by one we file out the door. The beauty of the day is a sweet relief after such a long and unpredictable winter. It's time to really look over the beds, shovel the rich and loamy compost on top of each, and begin planting some of those seeds and seedling varieties that can withstand the late spring cold snaps.

The French shallots that I planted in our first long bed have been standing tall above the surface for weeks now. Among them I find they're not the only eager growth.

The weeds have returned. With names akin to a Harry Potter novel, this season's weeds have come back in full vibrant growth. It doesn't take but a few seconds for me to be on my knees, pulling at the small roots.

Get them fast and get them young.

This is the principle for weeds. You don't wait. You don't put it off. You don't keep them around for decoration. You pull them as soon as they've spread their small green leaves. As soon as the soil can be worked, my fingers dig down a few inches and pull at whatever root I can find. Some pull out straight and clean. Some fight below the surface, snapping as I'm pulling, sure to return in a roaring vengeance in a few days. Some appear to thrive on their own. They're just small clusters of leaves from where I kneel, but when I pull at them, an entire network of roots and sprouts just below the surface move across the bed. Thin veins of destruction disrupt the entire surface of where I'm planting, the vines pulling loose from the earth for several feet.

"See this?" I say to my daughter, who is standing nearby watching as I work. "See how I pulled this one, singular weed and it was actually connected to all of these other things?" I say this in exasperation as the dirt flies through the air, roots and vines tangled in my hair, and it all falls on my now sweaty brow. As I'm saying this, it occurs to me how true this is. How important it is that I remember this. How vital this small weed is to understanding what work is happening in my own soul, where the dirt flies up and my fingers go raw.

See? That one, singular weed was connected to so many other things.

That one, miniscule weed was the lifeblood of hundreds of others.

*Spring*

That seemingly insignificant cluster of growth was hoping to take over the entire bed. Planning to ruin all of the healthy growth. Planning, intending, and virally growing in such a rapid way as to destroy all the good before I noticed its network just below the surface.

Maybe this is the biggest lie we believe—that sin isn't that bad. That when it is small, we can manage it. When it's tiny, seemingly insignificant, we think we can just leave it alone. How bad could it be? How destructive can such a small thing actually be?

And yet just beneath the surface, the small veins of festering growth stretch and divide, reach and cling. Next thing you know, something else pops up further away. Another small, innocuous and unrelated issue that seems to cause no major problems. Then another over here. A small annoyance over there. A heart slowly disrupted, slowly taken over, slowly emaciated by a hungry weed that wants to steal all the life, all the nutrients, all the water, all possibility of anything else thriving.

Today it's the bindweed that has enmeshed itself with the garden. I pull the network, disrupting the surface, pausing only to pull at other weeds with roots so deep; my bare hands won't be enough. To pull out those roots, I might have to dig up the entire bed, and that feels impossible; destroying a good thing in order to destroy a bad thing. Or can the garden even be truly good with a root system that feeds so far beneath the surface? To what degree am I willing to go to rid myself of this mess?

I am not ready. Today, I pull what I can with my gloved hands, weed tool, and small trowel. Today, I am doing my best to be diligent with what I know I have the grace to do. Tomorrow, I will return with a larger shovel, sharp tools, energy, maybe the help of my husband and some fortitude, and I will go after those roots. Maybe Jed will bring some ways to kill it, to choke them out with layers of cardboard, to starve them, to poison them, whatever we need to do. But we will be relentless, Lord willing.

Lord, make us relentless. Give us the energy to pull at the surface to see what's connected. To rid ourselves of hidden networks of sin that seek to steal, kill, and destroy. Give us the fortitude, the time, the heart, the sharp tools to dig beneath the surface to get to the root. And Lord, give us the courage to destroy what looks good and healthy in order to uproot what is sick and deadly.

Then when we're tired, sweating, and on our knees, remind us then that you can do the work even more thoroughly than we can.

You have sharper tools that pierce straight into the soul.

You once sweat in a garden so that when we're on our knees, digging in the dirt of our souls, we would look to you for obedience.

Your blood kills the roots we cannot reach.

Your strength outlasts ours.

Your grace suffocates that which steals our breath.

Your hands show us that you intend to finish the work you started in us.

*Spring*

## Cultivate

Identify the weeds you're fighting. Know them by name. Know what they look like. Crabgrass, lambsquarters, dandelion, knotweed, bindweed, nutsedge, broadleaf plantain, goosegrass, chickweed, creeping Charlie, horsetail, mugwort, smartweed. Sketch them, photograph them, then ruthlessly remove them. If you're not at the point of working in a garden, maybe do this same practice for your heart. Know the sins you're fighting. Name them. Know what they look like. See them, identify them, then ruthlessly remove them.

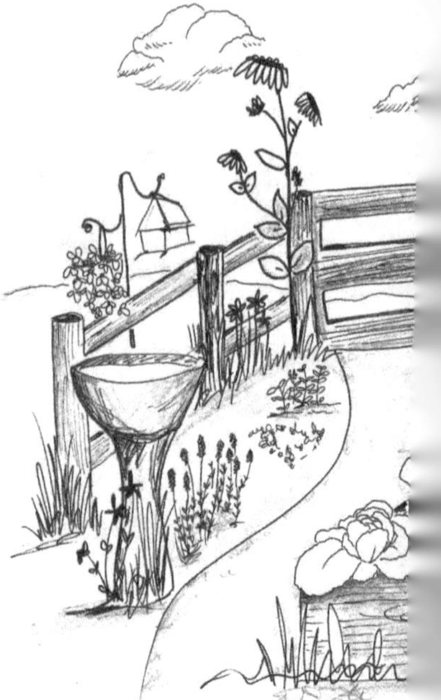

# SUMMER

25

# The War of the Weeds, *Part Two*

*To go to war in the garden is to humbly*
*go to war against yourself.*

*It's always the* same weeds. I promise you, if you pull it once from your garden, you will pull it fifty more times before the summer is over. Maybe not in the same bed or pot, but certainly the same variety. Weeds aren't that creative. Some have fooled me, no doubt. What I once thought was a bed of breadseed poppies turned out to be a patch of mugwort and, let me tell you, they are not nearly as exciting. By this time, your garden should be teeming with life. Growth, branches, flowers, climbing tendrils, and possibly even some early harvests to enjoy as the season really takes off. Yet the weeds clamor for your attention, too. It's tempting to ignore them. At first sight, they might seem relatively harmless. How bad could white goosefoot possibly be with a nursery rhyme name like that? But I promise you, they will invade.

Everything in the garden is in a silent competition for nutrients, water, sunlight, and space. Under the surface, the roots compete for the nutrients in the soil, crisscrossing along the subsoil pathways. Weeds are voracious and will steal what they can from whatever plant you are faithfully tending. Their stems will push right up alongside healthy plants, stealing their sunlight and the water that drips, and, perhaps, even growing so high as to create undesirable shade over your desired plants. They are quick to develop flowers and seeds because it ensures their survival. Some weeds twist their vines around a healthy plant, slowly choking the life out of a vegetable or flower, treating that stalk or stem as a mere means to survival. They will grow fast, close to the roots of the desired flora, close to the fruit, and become at minimum a nuisance and at worst a plant killer.

This is about when I remember that the work of tending creation was, at one time, a gift, but is now under the curse of Adam. The land doesn't gradually become healthier or more fruitful. It moves toward chaos and destruction. My work in the garden is a spiritual one. I am pushing back the darkness, taking dominion, and exercising my original design to tend, maintain, and keep the land.

So I will spend summer mornings before the sun is too hot bending over the beds to pull up whatever new weeds decided to creep up when I wasn't paying attention. It might take several looks at one bed for me to spot the mimicking leaves, but as the saying goes, once you see it, you can't unsee it. There have been

## 25 ⚜ The War of the Weeds, Part Two

years when I neglected portions of the garden only to let the weeds take over. Whether from exhaustion or feeling overwhelmed, the weeds lived in the periphery of both my garden and mind. Yet, the more I ignored them, the worse they got. Their puffy pods, sticky stems, burrs and wind-carried seeds started going everywhere in the garden. The problems I tried to ignore are now the only things I can see. What could have been solved earlier in the season became a grueling late summer project that was nearly impossible to fix. Tall weeds reached to the top and bent at the ceiling of my greenhouse where some straggling tomatoes tried to find the sun. My corn was completely choked out and produced small, immature cobs. The celery and cabbage that remained were hidden under the weeds that now claimed the dirt as home. The rose bush was hidden behind the green of marestail, which reached its near maximum height of more than five feet.

The gardener who delays weeding is only saying "yes" to an immeasurable amount of frustration, sweat, and likely failure, by the end of the harvest season. There is an old saying—the earliest I could find its appearance was in an old monthly publication from the 1800s—that says: "One year's seeding makes seven years' weeding." Essentially, if you let a weed go to seed, you will spend the next seven years of your life pulling that weed. Even more to the point: the weeds we accommodate become the weeds that kill us.

I try to explain this principle to my children. The delayed obedience, the deep-seated attitudes, the selfish bent we all have toward narcissism and making our own idols—these things can seem small and harmless at first. They seem almost too small to address. Too small to make an issue. So what if I'm feeling selfish in a certain area? I think of that scene from the movie version of *The Fellowship of the Ring* when Bilbo is holding the ring of power.

"After all, why not?" he asks. "Why shouldn't I keep it?"

I suppose I'm trying to warn you—the sins you accommodate become the sins that kill you. It's not a matter of "if" but "when." Pull them when they're small and see how the garden thrives. Wait until they're tall and see how the garden dies. Jesus knew this, warning us in the Parable of the Sower in Matthew 13: "Other seeds fell among thorns, and the thorns grew up and choked them."

We cannot expect to have abundant spiritual lives when we're also creating space for the things that will steal every nutrient, drop of water, ray of sunshine, and soil space it can find. Worldly distractions are not harmless. Sin is hungry. It does not care about the healthy life you're trying to grow. Kill it and do not delay any longer.

## Cultivate

Scout your garden for the weeds you need to pull. Do the hard work to save your crops before it's too late. If it helps, wait until just after a storm when the ground is still. Wait and you'll find it's easier to pull the roots out then. The rain soaks the ground, loosening the soil enough to make the roots of the weeds give way far more easily than they do during the dry days. This alone is enough to make me pause. As you work, remember Psalm 139:23–24:

## 25 ※ The War of the Weeds, Part Two

Search me, O God, and know my heart!
    Try me and know my thoughts!
And see if there be any grievous way in me,
    and lead me in the way everlasting!

## 26

# The All-Consuming Season

*Go to bed tired.*

*The birds started* singing before 4:30 a.m. this morning. I know this because I was awake, watching the sky turn from the dark black into that familiar dawn blue. The first bird sang bravely into the breaking morning light. While no sun rays had risen yet, her song made it clear that morning had arrived.

I'm awake because the needs and demands are heavy. The day stretches out before me in work that will inevitably wring me dry. The garden list, not one to be outdone, is running through my mind alongside every other weighty task today:

- Tie up the tomatoes.
- Harvest the peas.
- Pull the shallots.
- Check for potatoes.

- Weed the sweet potato bed.
- Cut the romaine for dinner.
- Pick the ripe cherries before the birds eat them all.
- Cut the last of the rhubarb.
- Collect the foxglove and lupine seeds.
- Thin the broom corn.

And I know it's just beginning. Next week, I will be checking for zucchini, curing more shallots, planting for the fall garden, and pulling the last of the spinach that has bolted, teaching the cucumber to climb, harvesting herbs, and so on. The work goes on until the first hard frost kills what remains. *Even then* winter will wrap her snow around the brussels, the kale, the last few carrots, and that persistent purple lettuce. From now until Christmas, I'll be watching this space from dawn until dusk, doing my best to not waste a harvest, an open soil patch, a window of time to gather as much as I can.

It's now only 4:33 a.m. and a part of me is already exhausted with the garden. The harvest is plentiful and the laborers are certainly few. It's me. That's it. I am the laborer. My husband is already rising to head off to work for the day, and I'll wrangle my kids to help as much as I can, but between my teenage daughter's vibrant social life and my six-year-old son's knack for pulling out "weeds," which are actually much-loved flowers, I tend to take on this daily task myself.

The harvest demands sweat. It demands early mornings, late nights, paper-cut fingertips from thorny weeds. It asks for my attention and my planning. It calls to me from my kitchen sink, the laundry room, from my office chair.

*It's ready, it's ready, it's ready. Harvest now.*

*It's ripe, go pick, it's sweet. Harvest now.*

*The sun is hot, the rain is scarce, today is the day before it's lost. Harvest now.*

The bird sings at dawn—*the morning is here, harvest before it's night again.*

It's all-consuming and I feel it pressing against my very hands. Here is when the plans I drafted in winter become the plans I rest my head on in summer. I know what I'm doing with each full basket. I know what is getting put up for the winter, what we're eating for dinner, and what goes where in that in-between. My fingerprints are caked with dirt, I smell of herbs and earth, and my muscles remind me each day of the work I have done.

The harvest is not a surprise. It is the most planned element of the entire garden. I can see how it all ends in an icy decay and so I'm working the field until the harvest sun sets. Until the birds go quiet again. Until I say goodnight to the garden.

The garlic and spinach beds will be repurposed as soon as I clear them—the fall vegetables will take their place. However, some beds will remain empty, allowing for them to rest before I plant again in the spring. Even the garden cannot be consumed year-round. Even the soil needs to sleep.

I remind myself of the joyful rest that comes for the one who labors intensely. Sleep is sweeter after sweat. We tell our children "Go to bed tired!" and this mantra is the one I live by in the season of harvest. Be ready to work.

In the church and in the community.

In the grocery stores and nursing homes.

In the pregnancy centers and after school programs.

In your own living room, online, your workspace, public transportation.

At the coffee shop where you see the same barista every day, the lunch spot with your favorite server, the grocery cashier who you recognize week after week.

With your children on the floor, your spouse at the dinner table, your parents at Christmas, your friends at brunch.

On a Sunday morning or a Tuesday night or a summer camp or Friday night prayer meeting. Be ready to join the joyful work.

Pray, ask, listen, share the hope of Christ.

Invite, feed, cry, hug, seek to show hospitality, and be the first to jump up when a need arises.

For wherever life is waking you up to the vibrant call of birdsong at dawn, be ready to be a laborer in the harvest fields. We should not be surprised; the Father knows the end and has called us to reap and reap until the harvest sun sets. So let's work the fields, brothers and sisters. Go to bed tired.

## Cultivate

Resist the urge to rest before the work is done. Find ways in your home, your church, your garden, or even a community garden, to be consumed entirely with hard work. Make a list of these things and find ways to joyfully say "yes" to as many good things as you can. Work the ground and the fields around you. Volunteer at church in a way you haven't served before. Sign-up to bring meals to new parents. Tackle that one garden bed that seems to nag at you every time you pass it. Harvest, preserve, put up, dehydrate, savor the season the garden is in. And find ways to do the same in your life. Let yourself be wrung out for those around you. The harvest is plentiful, and the laborers are few. Go to bed tired.

27

# Good Fences Make Good Neighbors

*Every man is sociable until a cow invades his garden.*

*Robert Frost first* made this sentiment known in his poem, "Mending Wall," though English scholar Oliver Tearle says this idea has shown up in literature as far back to the mid-1600s.[8] Anyone who has a garden, farm, field, or property will tell you that the boundary lines between us, even if they're invisible, aren't always created for isolation's sake and they do matter.

Property lines have always been an inherent limit for me. Growing up, it was the stone wall that divided our land from the Foxes' woods. The opposite line was the pond and the forbidden fields. Of course, only I called them the forbidden fields because they were the fields that belonged to the infamous Mrs. Grant.[9] Mrs. Grant was terrifying to me as a child. She had an almost fairy-tale-like lore about her, except in this story, she was the witch who probably ate children. She had even shot at two of our dogs, killing one of them. A rifle was perpetually strapped to her mailbox, held up by a dingy Bart Simpson doll. Her property stretched in odd ways, up the hill and toward the creek, and rumor had it the land was only hers because she had practically stolen it from her ex-husband during a nasty divorce. The family farmland that had been in his family for generations was where she now lived, slowly letting it sink into decrepitude. There is no happy ending here. Mrs. Grant terrorized all of her neighbors for years, thus creating an almost impenetrable bubble-like boundary line around her land and who she actually was as a person.

So it's true, the fields beyond our pond were the forbidden fields. They rolled green and grassy, but they were not really mine to roam.

As I've lived in different homes throughout my life, I've learned the importance and value of good boundaries and sturdy fences. Places the animals can roam, and the places they cannot. Places for public life; places for private life. Boundaries to roam; limits for where we should not go. People who can come close; those who cannot. I don't think it's a stretch to say that we can watch our Savior and see the same thing. Boundaries for who, when, what, and how he worked.

In the garden, knowing where to create these is essential. The chickens, for example, always want to get into the garden before it's time. There is a time and a place for chickens in the garden, but it's not in the middle of summer. It's certainly not when their scratching feet will rip out all that is vibrant and healthy. They have

## 27 ⁜ Good Fences Make Good Neighbors

no respect for the new growth, fresh vegetables, or carefully maintained pathways. They will dust-bathe right on top of your lisianthus seedlings without a care in the world. The deer are a delight to see in the field at early morning dawn. But they are significantly less lovely when they eat every sunflower head, ear of corn, and hosta leaf. Rabbits—adorable. Until you suddenly realize that you are Mr. McGregor chasing down Peter Rabbit who has eaten another batch of your nearly ripe tomatoes.[10] Imagine my snarky joy one day to see a rabbit or mouse had taken a rather large singular bite out of a bright red cayenne pepper. Good boundaries, including the right crop boundaries, help make good neighbors.

We have some cattle panels that are bent into an arch along a certain area of our garden. It's here every year that I plant our climbing flowers, climbing beans, and gourds that wind their way up the trellis. Our cucumbers are tucked underneath a hobbled together A-frame trellis. Our tomatoes are planted underneath a flat trellis that covers the entire bed. It's here where I'll tie the twine to the tomato base and then to the "ceiling" of the trellis, thus supporting the indeterminate tomatoes as they sprout up. All of these things act as boundaries for these plants. Grow this way, not that way. Grow up, not over. Stay close, don't stray.

Psalm 16:5–6 says,

> The LORD is my chosen portion and my cup;
>     you hold my lot.
> The lines have fallen for me in pleasant places;
>     indeed, I have a beautiful inheritance.

I remind my plants of this when I tie them up to the trellis, weave them through a net, knot the twine. The boundary lines have fallen for you in pleasant places. This is what's best for you. It's better for every animal and human on our property to have those boundary lines, and for them to realize they are in the right spot. Maybe this is why it sometimes feels so unnatural to us as humans when someone asks us to tie ourselves to a place we certainly can't exist. Social media asks this of us every single day.

"Tie yourself up here! Climb here! Trellis here!" when in reality we're planted in another plot, another place, behind other fences or forbidden fields. We simply cannot exist everywhere.

When I think that God has put me in a city or state that just doesn't seem like the right place, I remember—the lines have fallen for me in pleasant places.

When I want to be more successful, wealthy, known, or admired—the lines have fallen for me in pleasant places.

When I don't get answers to all of my prayers, when my hopes wither away, when the answer is "no" or "not right now"—the lines have fallen for me in pleasant places.

I can trust the Lord when he says, "Go up; not across." Or "Climb here, not there." Or "Those fields are not yours to roam." He can see what I cannot—the threats, the dangers, the health, the growth. When I feel trellised, tied, knotted, held back, fenced in, hemmed in, limited, or kept out—the boundaries are not a punishment but a careful hand of the Good Shepherd.

So as I weave the vine of the gourds through the cattle panels today and shoo a chicken out of the garden paths, I remember that there is a beautiful place and boundary for all things so that we can all love one another well. Good fences make good neighbors, even out of me.

## Cultivate

Plan ahead to provide good boundaries for your garden. Will you need tall deer fencing or would a low wattle fence do the trick? Utilize the vertical space of your garden by providing trellises and places for your climbing plants to climb. Garden structures and good fences will bring a measure of peace and order to your garden. Certainly, some critters might bite their way through the fence, but you'll have a better chance of keeping them at bay if you start with a barrier before you even plant. We even bury our deer fencing six-to-twelve inches into the ground to try and deter any animals that might attempt to dig under the fence.

As you consider the ways to protect and provide good boundaries in your garden, consider where you feel limited and held back in your own day to day life. Where has God said "no"? Where have the boundary lines fallen for you? Write a prayer of gratitude for the places you have found the boundaries of God that keep you from forbidden fields or wasted energy.

## 28

# The Pruning Season

*The sheep are tended by the shepherd's crook,
the branches by the pruning hook.*

*There are few things* more painful to a gardener than the first pruning. The clip of the shears against that David Austin rose or dahlia bud feels so unnatural. There is an old lilac on the corner of our barn and it has likely been growing there since the first farmer broke ground in this soil more than one hundred and thirty years ago. The spring after we moved, after the lilac bloomed and shed its petals, my husband took our hedge trimmer to the green branches that had stretched in undesirable places. It needed shaping and care, but my initial reaction was to completely lose my mind that he had chopped it back so significantly. I thought it was done. I was convinced he had ruined one of the true beauties of our property. Naturally, some googling calmed my fears a bit, but it wasn't until the following spring that I truly had to apologize and tell him I was completely wrong.

The tree was lush, bathed in purple blooms, filling our yard with the desirable scent. The smell of the lilac tree takes the prize in my opinion and that spring we had all of the prizes. Every limb seemed to have a bloom to cut.

Lilacs grow their new blooms sometime in the summer. Yes, that's right. The ones that won't bloom for another nine months—they take their initial form in the summer. New blooms also form off of pruned branches. The blooms will fill the end of every branch that gets lopped off, ensuring the survival and seed of that tree for the next year. So as it turns out, pruning is exactly what the lilac needed for optimal growth. It's what a lot of things need for optimal growth, if only we have the guts and the heart to do the work.

Depending on the variety, some roses need to be pruned as well. This will allow for new, healthy stems to burst forth in the spring, bringing with them the desired poetic flora. Hydrangeas, butterfly bush, azalea, perennial flowers like foxglove, salvia, peonies, astilbe, iris, and so many others do well with a good seasonal pruning. The trick is knowing when. Pruning at the wrong time could kill or destroy whatever bloom you're hoping to have. The best advice I can give in this small space is to research and know your garden. You are the only one who knows what your garden truly needs. Plan to prune at least twice a year, in spring and summer, for the different flowers and bushes growing on your property. This work also helps prevent disease and rot and other issues from growing within your beds. Don't compost these clippings—toss them into a fire, into the trash, or into the woods.

But here's the honest truth—after years of gardening, I am still not a confident pruner. Even after researching down to every last detail, I am scared I will kill something I love. I'm also prone toward exhaustion. There are times I know I should prune, for example, the row of peonies that need my attention. But I'm weary and the days fill with other louder and more demanding things and even this task gets pushed to the bottom of the list. As much as I love gardening and as hard as I try to be faithful to work, I can still fail at things that really would make the entire garden better.

This is likely why I get so terrified when I feel the Father's pruning shears pressed against parts of me I hold dear. Things that I'm tempted to believe make me who I am. A lifelong dream. A creature comfort. A coping mechanism. In John 15:2, Jesus actually tells us that if we're bearing fruit, we should expect pruning to stay healthy. This isn't shocking. This is good husbandry. This is faithful gardening. This isn't punishment. Quite the opposite. It is his present and tender care. A promise of better things.

When I feel the pruning shears against the fruitful edges of my own heart, I wince, knowing that something that feels like it's a part of me is about to get lopped off for good. I'm tempted to believe my Father is angry at me, or worse, disappointed in me. Is the Vinedresser simply trying to humiliate my joy and put in me my place?

## 28 ❦ The Pruning Season

None of this is true. The Father, the Vinedresser—he doesn't do sloppy work. He doesn't put pruning on the bottom of the list as I do. He doesn't work in the wrong season or at the wrong time. He's never exhausted with the detailed work that is required in me. He's not worried he's going to kill me; he's trying to put to death the things in me that keep me from staying truly alive.

Every year, my flower farming friend Ashley grows dahlias. Stunning, show-stopping blooms. When the season is thriving, they are a sight to behold. But she also has to do the work of pinching them when they are growing tall and healthy. This is what you do for dahlias. One by one, cutting back the seemingly healthy growth. Why? Because this forces the dahlia to send out more shoots. More shoots equals more blooms. And who doesn't want more blooms?

"It's time to pinch the dahlias," she'll say with a sigh and some trepidation. We all know it's necessary but it always comes with a pang. In a smaller way, this is what happens when we remove the deadheads of flowers during the growing season. As soon as they're gone, the plant knows it's time to make more. Remove what needs to be removed—trust that the work matters.

Let me reassure you—the Father is not nervous with his sharp pruning hook. Whatever he removes from us is only and always for the good. He's mindful of the disease that rots away inside of our bones, our stems, and our branches. He can see our potential—what we can be, will be, could be—if only we would submit ourselves to his trustworthy hands.

> The sheep are tended by the shepherd's crook,
> the branches by the pruning hook.

## Cultivate

Research what plants you have that need pruning and mark your calendars for when this will need to occur. Have a pair of sharp and clean pruners ready to cut when the time comes. Consider designing your garden in such a way that you have some to prune in the spring and some in the fall.

## 29

# The Hidden Fruit

*Look under.*

"Look under," I tell my children again and again. "Look under, look under." These words are familiar to them when we're harvesting any fruit or vegetable. This is my humming song as I lift branch after branch.

Whether it be blueberries, strawberries, the first fat peas of the season, or the peppers that curve around their sturdy spines. The best fruit is hidden. The blueberries are in plump clusters just underneath the green bough. The strawberries are tucked under the green leaves, in the straw, fattened with juice. The fattest peas are the ones we pass over on the first picking. The longest beans are the ones we won't even find for a few weeks. Even the pumpkins hide underneath their own leafy umbrellas until one day we feel we've stumbled into the fairy godmother's patch.

This is the best encouragement to me from the garden: the most abundant fruit is found in the places no one is really looking. I spend my weeks working for my church, in the office, on phone calls, in meetings, facing crisis after crisis, pouring my heart into discipleship material and studies and emails, and most days it looks like I'm not producing much fruit. When I'm not at church, I'm home, pouring into these four walls and these lives, emptying every last drop of my soul into animated voices during read aloud time, exhausting my arms to roll out homemade tortillas for taco night, vacuuming up copious amounts of dog hair, or washing the next pile of dishes or laundry. The garden is just the next place this happens. Days, weeks, months, sometimes years of work ... for what? I get the occasional, "You know there's a grocery store just down the road, right?" and I laugh, but really *what am I doing? Does any of this matter?*

The work of simply living often feels like futility. Washing one load of laundry so we can wear the very clothes we will make dirty and have to wash again. Correcting one of my children only for them to forget and do it again in about three minutes. Cooking dinner only to fill the sink with more dishes that I'll need to use for another meal in the morning. Another church meeting where someone decides they're going to pursue their sin instead of repentance. The redundancy on repeat, day in and day out. A full Ecclesiastes moment hits me, and the long haul feels long without much harvest to haul.

Is it the kindness of the Lord when I lift a heavy leaf to find a deep red pepper hiding in the shadow? Yes, absolutely it is. In each handful of berries or tomatillos, long and ripe cucumbers or football-sized zucchinis, I remember that God's faithfulness is not usually attended by a crowd of onlookers and applause. It's usually hidden. Deep in a manger, a weeping Savior alone in a garden, a rolling stone at dawn.

Recently, on a warm July night, we had some friends over for some grilled steak, vegetables, and roasted potatoes. We sat around the table outside in the late evening sun and realized that everything we were eating was grown within a ten-mile radius—even the cow! I had just harvested the potatoes that day. We grow a certain variety of purple potato that looks almost fake. In fact, when it's raw and you cut it open, it resembles a geode, glimmering in the light. One of our friends pointed out that the potato came straight from our garden, which mesmerized the children who were paying attention.

"Do you want to pick some?" I asked, and in a matter of minutes, I was leading a train of curious children and their parents to the potato bed.

"It's like treasure hunting," I told them. "You have to be willing to dig your hands in the ground, get dirty, and feel for potatoes." Within twenty minutes, boys and girls alike were filthy and still as happy as they could be—and, to my delight, my wood crate was full.

Look under. Be willing to get dirty. Have the faith of a child.

I am learning to pay attention to the shadowed and hidden spaces. I am learning to be patient and take my time during the harvest. I am learning to dig and seek and find. I'm learning to lift the branches and trust that the harvest is not up to me to produce—only to gather. Fill my crates, Lord. I'll be ready.

## Cultivate

Pause here in your busy life. Pour a cup of tea, a fresh cup of coffee, or fill a tall glass with ice cold lemonade. Reflect for a moment on the world that surrounds you, that at times might feel as if it is outpacing you, and demanding your energy with what seems like little payoff. The futility of life is an invitation to despair, until we pause and look under. Read the following passage aloud and take a moment to think on what it means for your life, then respond to God in prayer:

> What gain has the worker from his toil? I have seen the business that God has given to the children of man to be busy with. He has made everything beautiful in its time. Also, he has put eternity into man's heart, yet so that he cannot find out what God has done from the beginning to the end. I perceived that there is nothing better for them than to be joyful and to do good as long as they live; also that everyone should eat and drink and take pleasure in all his toil—this is God's gift to man.
>
> I perceived that whatever God does endures forever; nothing can be added to it, nor anything taken from it. God has done it, so that people fear before him. That which is, already has been; that which is to be, already has been; and God seeks what has been driven away. (Ecclesiastes 3:9–15)

30

# The Mimic Weeds

*Let both grow together until the harvest, and at harvest time I will tell the reapers, "Gather the weeds first and bind them in bundles to be burned, but gather the wheat into my barn."*

*I* am ashamed to admit this, but if I am going to be honest, I must tell you about the poppies and the campanula.

Each spring and summer, as the beds of my garden fill up, I leave certain spots untouched where I know the usual suspects will return. The tansy, the rudbeckia, the celosia, the calendula, and yes, the poppies and campanula. There is a portion of one bed, on the north side of the field, that I carefully marked for the poppies and campanula. I watched as green leaves unfolded in the spring and told my kids and husband, "Watch out there! Those are the poppies!" or "I can't wait to see the Canterbury bells (campanula) this year!" Everything in the garden began to grow and seeds were started and planted, and before I knew it, a solid two months had passed before something occurred to me.

That entire northern end of the bed had neither poppies nor campanula blooming. In fact, it had no flowers at all. As my newly planted poppies bloomed in other beds, I realized that my protected and nurtured bed was barren of beauty. So I went to investigate what had gone wrong, and saw the truth towering in front of me. That was not a poppy stem. I knew it as soon as I paid enough attention to what I was actually looking at. That was mugwort. That was a bed of tall weeds. An entire half of a garden bed, full of nurtured and protected *weeds*.

As someone who has gardened for more than a few years, I certainly do not consider myself a complete amateur. And this was an amateur's mistake. I admitted this to my gardening friends in laughter—I had spent months apparently mindlessly and ignorantly tending ... weeds.

Foxtail, a highly invasive weed that mimics grass and other well-loved crops, also can occasionally have red stems at its base. Which is good to know when it grows right next to the red onions in the onion bed. Ask me how I know.

There is a weed which has made its way into what could only be considered garden and farming lore at this point called darnel. While most of it has been eradicated from our modern crops, it was considered a true mimic weed, growing among the wheat and depending on the wheat for its deceptive survival.[11] It was in fact darnel that the enemy sowed among the wheat in the parable of the weeds in Matthew 13:24–30. Darnel looks so similar to wheat that it was impossible to know which was which until harvest time. To remove the darnel would mean potentially harming the wheat harvest. I've seen this damage occur when I have pulled weeds that grow right next to the flowers and vegetables. Sometimes they grow so closely together that to remove the weed would essentially uproot the entire plant. In some cases, I have left the weed or cut it back until the established plant was mature enough to handle some root disruption.

It can be difficult to spot the mimic weeds for what they are until they have grown up among your harvest. Some botanists have suggested that these weeds have adapted to their neighboring plants, evading elimination by simply looking like the real thing. Think of it this way: once these weeds go to seed, those characteristics that spared them the first time around will now get passed on to the next generation. In time, those weeds that look the most like the things we eat and cut for flowers will only persist. It is up to the gardener and farmer to weed early, or to find ways to separate the final results in the harvest.

Otherwise, we might find we are staring at mugwort when we were hoping for poppies. Or that we have Queen Anne's Lace instead of carrots. Or darnel and not wheat.

It's humbling to realize I've been duped. When I discover that a true friend was actually a mimic. When fruit I thought was growing in my heart wasn't the real thing at all. (Like the time I tried giving up coffee and I realized that I'm not really a kind and patient person; I'm just caffeinated.) When I think about that final day when I stand before Christ, I wonder how much of me, my life, my ministry, my work will actually remain and how much will burn into ashes as the false thing that it was. It's all tainted with my pride, my ego, my selfishness. Even the garden.

But there is the sweet joy of harvesting, when the weeds are finally tossed to the side and I discover that underneath the foxtail stems, the onions grew much bigger than I realized. Their fruitfulness was not marred by the fake that grew next to them. They just grew. And I suppose there's something in this for us too—for the work of ministry, friendships, living in this world—the best thing we can do is simply mind our own affairs and work with our hands, as Thessalonians calls us to do. Live a quiet life. The mimic weeds will not make it to the end. But we can trust that the Gardener, on that last day, will wield his winnowing fork with such skill, we will wonder why we ever doubted at all.

## Cultivate

There are times when there isn't much you can do about the mimics. You know they are not going to produce anything useful or beneficial, and yet to move them would disrupt the bed entirely, roots and all.

Get a sharp pair of garden shears and go straight for the base of their stems at the surface of the ground. If you cannot uproot them, at least take away the girth of their life. This will, at minimum, slow down their pervasiveness among your plants. At the end of the season, pull out the root ball before you shut the garden down for the year.

The same diligence can be applied in our daily lives. Where we cannot uproot something entirely, let's not grow apathetic toward its existence. Remove its life. Suffocate it, stifle it, do all you can to mark it, and let the Master Gardener do the final work. He who began a good work in us is faithful to complete it (Philippians 1:6).

## 31

# The Storms of Destruction

*Jesus! what a Guide and Keeper!*
*While the tempest still is high,*
*storms about me, night o'ertakes me,*
*He, my Pilot, hears my cry.*
*Hallelujah! what a Savior!*
*Hallelujah! what a Friend!*
*Saving, helping, keeping, loving;*
*He is with me to the end.*

*I thought I was* prepared for the high winds, but my trellises were not, evidently. They fell sideways, taking with them half of my beans and a few precious flowers as well. The same storm is the one that took down some beloved sunflowers of a friend of mine. She had been patiently waiting for the seven-foot-tall sunflowers to bloom, but just before they did, the winds came and cracked their stalks, sending the heavy, nearly-open blooms to the ground.

## 31 ❀ The Storms of Destruction

I've heard of hail that destroys pumpkins, ripping through their leaves and pummeling the large ripening fruits to smithereens. An intense thunderstorm whipped through our region last year, and a family down the road had a massive tree collapse right on top of their garden beds. The whole garden was destroyed in one tree's demise. During a gusty spring storm in 2020, right during family movie night, the old maple tree that stood at the corner of our house fell on top of our porch roof, shattering an upstairs window and put the fear of God in each of us who were gathered in the living room. These stories don't even scratch the surface for those who keep watch with radar and weather channels for funnel clouds, floods, derechos, and larger-than-life hail. As beautiful and exciting as a good old summer thunderstorm might be, the potential for irrevocable damage is just behind the edge of the storm.

When I was a kid, I wanted to be a storm chaser. Of course, I said this from the safety of my home in upstate New York, having never experienced tornado weather. I watched *Twister* once and decided I wanted to be as cool as Helen Hunt and Bill Paxton. In my twenties, I ended up moving to Texas for a few years. That's when I had my first real taste of those southern storms and, let me tell you what, I was not itching to get in my car and follow them. I spent a few storms in an underground tornado shelter (it was actually an unused septic tank buried in the ground with a ladder. I am still alive, so it can't be that bad of an idea.) I spent an hour or two huddled in a tub, and once or twice in a basement. Once, when I was driving home, I noticed that the sky had turned that strange color and things were moving suspiciously. I missed that tornado touchdown by just a few minutes and a few miles. Ironically, it was in Texas that the Lord allowed the work of my own destruction to completely gut me and humble me on my face. In Hosea 8:7, Hosea prophesies: "For they sow the wind and they shall reap the whirlwind." As one who once sowed wind and chaos in my life, reaping the whirlwind was exactly what happened.

Storms have the power to destroy, but under the sovereign hand of God, they still cannot steal what he has preserved for his own. Storms will inevitably come and some will refresh the ground, bringing with them the peace that only a good summer storm can bring. But some will uproot things that you certainly thought would never be moved. You might even find that some things are uprooted and damaged in such permanent ways that your heart and spirit go right out from you.

The storm that tore through my hometown years ago literally rewrote roads and maps. Entire homesteads were flooded with mud and debris. A threat of a dam collapse seemed imminent. Fishing boats traveled down new rivers that were once roads. The small-town library I frequented as a child, in that old yellow Victorian house, was flooded with twenty-seven inches of mud, wiping out shelves of books. In my memory, I can still see the photos of the street that I used to walk in my high school years with my friends, with the road's shoulders piled with seven feet or more of destroyed furniture, beds, entire houses with entire lifetimes, ready to be

## 31 ❦ The Storms of Destruction

hauled off to the landfill. The storm destroyed. A whirlwind of desolation.

While so many worked hard to rebuild and restore all that the storm had taken, there were some who simply couldn't recover. Businesses and homes were boarded up and remain empty to this day. Certain roads are still impassable.

Some storms bring peace, but the brutality of others cannot be withstood. Our hopes, our dreams, our plans, our finances, our pride, our image, and sometimes even our faith is uprooted, flooded, piled high in rubbish, and we wonder if there is anything worth rebuilding again.

Yet the trellises can be nailed together. The places where trees once stood now sit as reminders of the magnitude of suffering. The shattered windows can be restored. The ruined harvests will be wept over, and we will plant again. The roads might be impassable, and while it might take years and new maps, we will find another way. The houses are boarded up, but we will find a new home. The books might be destroyed, but we can write new ones.

God's grace to his children doesn't ask us to live in misery, only viewing suffering as a final verdict on our lives. In fact, because of Christ, we know that our final verdict is the opposite of destruction—it is new roots, new growth, restoration, redemption, and maybe even the kind of hope that still flickers in the dark.

The kind of faith that shows up early on a Sunday morning at the grave of a dead man, bidding us to be faithful, even when all seems lost. The kind of faith that gives us strength to endure until we hear the voice of the Gardener at last.

## Cultivate

If possible, know the general direction of the storm winds for your property. We cannot protect against any and all unforeseen storm systems, but we can gird the gardens up against the things we can predict. Our spring and summer storms usually blow in from the west and we can watch them as they turn the skies over the lake a dark slate gray. I know the winds will whip a certain way when things build. This is why we do our best to anchor our structures in the garden. We cannot stop the storms that are destructive in force, but we can do what we can to be anchored deeper than just the surface.

The storms of life are no more predictable. We might know the general direction of some problems but the likelihood of predicting every threat is impossible. We cannot protect every physical and tangible thing we have in our lives. For someone like me who struggles to fight fear, this reality is sometimes difficult to stomach. No one person can guarantee that our material belongings, our loves, and our bodies will come out unscathed. And so, in whatever small faith I can muster at times, I anchor whatever structures exist in my life deep below the surface. As Corrie ten Boom is famous for saying: "Never be afraid to trust an unknown future to a known God." His invitation is to anchor ourselves so deep within his foundations that even when the storms come—and

## 31 ❦ The Storms of Destruction

they will—we are not necessarily unshaken but we are faithfully anchored when everything shakes. He is what holds us. So with each hammer on the trellis, I am reminded that the anchoring work of Christ is deeper, more secure, and reaches unseen places.

> Everyone then who hears these words of mine and does them will be like a wise man who built his house on the rock. And the rain fell, and the floods came, and the winds blew and beat on that house, but it did not fall, because it had been founded on the rock. (Matthew 7:24–25)

## 32

# After the Storm

*Sow for yourselves righteousness;*
*reap steadfast love;*
*break up your fallow ground,*
*for it is the time to seek the* Lord,
*that he may come and rain righteousness upon you.*

*We have waited* for this storm. For weeks now, the air has been thick with humidity to the point where I almost feel I could wring the air out like a dishrag. I've watered the garden as much as I can but it seems pointless. The air sucks it right back up. Even the slightest movement is heavy laden and I am sweating before I take two steps out of my door. Leaves are limp, everything wilts a bit, including us humans. Each day, the forecast calls for rain, but the storms disappear by the afternoon and never come to fruition. It's the topic of all small talk.

"Really ready for some rain, huh?"

## 32 ※ After the Storm

"Boy, it's pretty humid out there, isn't it?"

"I'm tired of sweating—think it'll rain today?"

We watch the horizon as the clouds thicken and turn gray, but somehow, they dissipate again. No relief, no rain; another day of dishrag dewpoints.

And then there's the thick afternoon, when a distant rumble rattles across the treetops. My six-year-old son perks up his head from where he's digging for bugs.

"Was that thunder?"

A gray and black shadowed line of thunderheads billow toward the west. A towering white thunderhead looms bright above the sideways winds that are already flipping the leaves over. This can only mean one thing—today we will get rain. I nod and he runs inside as fast as he can, ready to find a spot on the porch to watch the storm roll in.

The relief that comes after a summer storm is palpable. As if the whole earth breathes a sigh of relief for a moment. The grass bounces back green, the sky unfolds in a majestic display of color, and rain drips from each plant leaf like something out of a Disney movie.

If you're wondering the best time to pull your weeds: this is it. A good soaking rain makes the ground give up the weeds in surrender. The roots slip out and other plants remain largely untouched by the disturbance. I will willingly drench good pants, church clothes, leather shoes, you name it to take advantage of a good post-storm weeding session.

This is the joyful relief that the storm brings. The birds return, singing and hopping around the yard in cartoon-like fashion. They splash in the birdbath and flutter about on the tops of the sunflowers in song. In a great chorus of worship, all of creation praises the God who sustains his earth, sending seed for the sower and bread for the eater, sending rain and snow, sending forth his word that does not return to him void. Even the worms and frogs will come out to praise.

Run to your garden just as the storm has passed. Lift your head to see the rolling edge of the thunderstorm as it moves away. Look for the rainbow that is likely stretched somewhere nearby, pointing at the heart of heaven. Bend low and weed. Drench your best clothes just to smell the scent of the soil as it opens up again.

This joyful peace is the closest I can compare to the work of the gospel. The first time the words of a pastor jumped out at me with gospel, Christ-centered truth, I turned to my friend and said: "If this is true, this is really, really good news." She laughed and said something like *that's kinda the point.* The same exuberant joy fills my heart after the storm and the garden is brought back to life, back to growth and green. Is the storm over? If this is true, this is really, really good news. Did the storm break up the fallow ground? If this is true, this is really, really good news. Do the birds sing for it? The flowers glisten because of it? Does the whole earth give thanks for it? Yes, because the storm has come and the storm has passed. This is really, really good news.

It's hard to know how thirsty you are until you start drinking water.

## 32 ※ *After the Storm*

It's hard to know how dirty you are until the water washes over you.

We are not good gauges of our own need for the gospel. In fact, I'd say the very small measure of awareness we do have is only a hint at how needy we are. We need the gospel to resurrect us; to shake us with thunder and drench us with salvation. God, open the ground so we can pull out the mess.

### Cultivate

Reflect on a storm in your own personal life. This could be either metaphorical or real. Write a prayer to give thanks for the storm, praise to the one who has control over the storms, and an honest prayer for how it ended. Pray through Isaiah 45:5–8 and Psalm 148:7–8:

> I am the LORD, and there is no other,
>   besides me there is no God;

Lord God, you are the Lord and there is no other. You alone hold all things in your hands. In each season of storms, help me to look to you and you alone for all things.

> I equip you, though you do not know me,
> that people may know, from the rising of the sun
>   and from the west, that there is none besides me;

Lord, you have made us and sustain all things for your glory. You hold the sun's rising and setting in your hands. You give us all we need before we even ask. You have made all things to proclaim your goodness and faithfulness.

> I am the LORD, and there is no other.
> I form light and create darkness;
> I make well-being and create calamity;
> I am the LORD, who does all these things.

You create the things we depend on. You are sovereign. You have not lost control and will never lose control over your creation.

> Shower, O heavens, from above,
> and let the clouds rain down righteousness;
> let the earth open, that salvation and righteousness may bear fruit;
> let the earth cause them both to sprout;
> I the LORD have created it. (Isaiah 45:5–8)

In my humanity and creatureliness, help me to stand openhanded under the work you do in my life. Keep me from attempting to wrangle control and power from you. Forgive me for forgetting your magnificence and majesty. Let your rain wash over me so that salvation and righteousness may bear fruit in me. May the ground I work be a small fruit of praise to you for who you are.

> Praise the LORD from the earth,
> you great sea creatures and all deeps,
> fire and hail, snow and mist,
> stormy wind fulfilling his word! (Psalm 148:7–8)

## 33

# The Garden Pests

*There are some things in this world that certainly must have been distorted after the fall of Eden—mosquitoes for one.*

*The first sight* of the Japanese beetle is the most dreaded day of the garden season. If you haven't yet become acquainted with this indomitable pest, consider yourself under a special umbrella of God's kindness because they are the bane of every gardener's existence. In fact, there's a commiseration that occurs when the first friend texts a photo of one of these dreaded scarabs chomping away at a beloved rose or hollyhock leaf. Once you see them, it feels like the beginning of the end. From that point on, it will be a battle. Last summer, we filled a bucket with hot, soapy water and I sent my two children out to pluck each beetle they could find off the branches and drown them in the suds. This lasted for a solid ten minutes, until they both came in breathless, telling me a vine-covered garden fence was covered with hundreds of beetles who swarmed them when they hit the fence.

I asked my six-year-old, "Why did you hit the fence?" He had no good answer. Curiosity killed the beetle evictions that day.

If it's not the Japanese beetles that devour precious leaves, flowers, and food, it's definitely the other ones.

The squash bugs (in my opinion, the second worst invaders of the garden) will lay clusters of brown eggs that can be spotted on squash and pumpkin leaves. If they are removed, you have at least managed the first batch. The problem is when you realize you've missed one small birth, and your squash leaves and gourds are overwhelmed with tiny, gray bugs that scurry around like the stuff of nightmares. They disgust me, and this year I sacrificed a small pumpkin to them in hopes they would leave the rest alone.

The tomato hornworms, squash vine borers, potato beetles, all other kinds of slugs, caterpillars, aphids, beetles, and cabbage worms are the dark underbelly of garden life. It is a race, or rather a war, against time. Against disease and devoured crops. Against rotted out potatoes and slimy pumpkins. Against lace-like leaves and black rotted roses that never bloomed. Cabbage with tunnels and green dung piles, carrots with holes that climb all the way through, tomatoes that fall from the vine before they're even red, zinnias that have been chewed to pieces.

I once heard Theresa Loe on her podcast *Living Homegrown* talk about how the spiders were the real police of the garden. They eat most things and ward off the worst of the invaders, devouring all kinds of bugs in the garden beds. I always make sure to greet whatever spider is weaving her web under my vegetables because she really is in this with me. Neither of us want her to be indoors.

Here are my top tips for those garden pests:

1. Identify them by name. Know where they live, what their eggs look like, what the hatched larvae look like, and what they look like as adults.

2. As soon as you see one, kill it. Do not pause, do not hesitate, do not think, "But, oh! It's so cute and harmless." Remove it. In some cases, like Japanese beetles, the bugs send out early scouts to find where to feast. If you can catch them before the whole family moves in, you have a better chance of eradicating them. Or at least lessening their presence that year.

3. Some neem oil spray blends work great or you can make your own from a neem oil based concentrate. This is one natural way to remove some pests. It's not perfect but it is organic and safe for your vegetables and flowers. I personally have never tried diatomaceous earth but that also comes highly recommended to help deter the unwanted bugs.

4. I've had great luck drowning many a pest in a bucket of hot soapy water. The viscosity of the fluid is enough to keep them from resurfacing and flying away. Dump

these far away from the garden though. Sometimes the scent of dead bugs will just attract more.

5. Plant companion plants that deter the worst pests. Many herbs such as dill, oregano, rosemary, and mint will work as bug repellents in your garden beds. My personal favorite to plant is nasturtium. It repels many bugs, is lovely to look at, and every part of the nasturtium plant is edible. Planting celery with cabbage or broccoli is another example of this. Celery deters the white cabbage moth which will eat your brassicas out of house and home. The years I've done this, I'm always amazed to see how healthy my cabbage heads grow in the shadow of the celery leaves.

6. Research creative ideas. The internet is full of solutions: cinnamon to deter slugs, placing bird feeders close to the garden, cayenne pepper spray, and so on. There is no shortage of people who are on your side, trying to figure this out with you. I'm one of them.

We may never be free entirely from the pests in the work that we do, but we can at least become experts on them. While there are certainly ways to eradicate bugs (and I would suggest doing thorough research before just buying any garden bug spray you find at the store), the reality is that this is part of the garden. You will never have a pest-free experience, especially since some of the

## 33 ※ The Garden Pests

pests are actually killing the other bugs you don't want and so you learn to give thanks for things like spiders, wasps, and midges. The diligence to remove them can feel exhausting. Since one of the works of the Spirit of God in us is to sanctify us, I imagine it's an awful lot like pinching off squash bug eggs under every single leaf. To miss one cluster of eggs could mean the complete destruction of that crop. To passively skip removal could mean a passive choice of destruction. Eradicating tiny issues is no small thing. They have to be drowned, killed, squished, sprayed, pinched, fed to the chickens, you name it. But they cannot stay here. Part of our work in imaging God in both creation and in the active work in each other's lives is to push back darkness. Sometimes darkness is obvious and big; sometimes it lays eggs in tiny, hidden places. Someone needs to do the work of turning over the leaves. Crushing the things that seem harmless. Drowning the first sign of something that will destroy me. Know its name at every stage. Be relentless.

### Cultivate

What have you allowed to live in your soul, thinking it harmless? Identify them by name. Know what they look like at all stages. Know what damage they cause, where they hide, and how you've adapted your life to make room for these seemingly harmless pests.

Bring community into this work. Give permission to those you trust around you to pinch off those bugs as soon as they surface. A good friend points out the roaches. A good friend hits the fence when they see the swarm gathering. Learn to companion plant relationships in your life. If you struggle with something specific, get a friend who doesn't struggle the same way. Find someone who isn't afraid to be different, say no, or reject that particular temptation.

# 34

# The Heat

*Endurance requires abiding in Christ, even when the conditions around you try to convince you that you ought to try living somewhere else.*

As I write this, I am sitting at my in-law's house in the middle of July in Vermont. The summer heat is predicted to roar over the eastern seaboard, which for us means a humid and thick day in the mid-nineties. We're spending our afternoon talking about the lake, what time we'll arrive at Bomoseen, planning out a hot July day of canoeing, swimming, hot dogs and burgers, and the kind of summer days I hope my kids remember for the rest of their lives. But, good heavens, it's hot. Sweat constantly accumulating on my upper lip and dripping down my back kind of hot. Here on the dry Vermont hillside, each car traveling up the mountain sends up clouds of dust from the road. It lingers in the air long enough to cast a fog-like hue over all our outdoor activities for a few minutes.

"We need rain," my mother-in-law says as the clouds billow over the house. She points out the purple flowers that bend sadly on her front patio. "They shrivel up in this kind of heat," she sighs. They were beautiful but the heat suffocates the joy out of them until they're wimpy mimics of what they could be. Heat does this. Heat of the sun, heat of the fire, heat of life. Heat that puts your feet to a flame and makes you long for water, for refreshing, for any kind of relief. In the heat my poppies faint, my cool weather crops bolt to flower as fast as can be, and I watch the forecast for the next sign of rain. I remember the days of Texas heat when I lived there—a constant feeling of walking through a dry furnace, moving from air-conditioned room to air-conditioned room to whatever air-conditioned space you could find next.

There is little respite for the flowering plant or heat-intolerant vegetable once these days hit. I'll water in the morning before the sun rises above the treeline in hopes the ground will absorb as much as possible before the air claims it all for itself. Summer heat makes me long for cold, winter days. I can't remember now what snow feels like, what frost looks like on the windows, what the wind sounds like when it howls around the eaves.

*Except. However. But.*

There is nothing in God's redemptive creation that doesn't produce fruitfulness somehow. This is the holy economy; nothing wasted, faithfulness in the suffering, life out of the ashes. So here in the dry beds, where the flowers faint, there are some things that are abundantly happy.

The sweet potatoes stretch wide and joyfully. The peppers breathe a sigh of relief. The onions that are ready to be cured take a sunbath under the heat. The cosmos and geraniums unfold in happy color. Coneflower, marigold, zinnia, yucca – each one seems to thrive when the days are hot and the storms are short, or not at all. I might be wilting, but they are not.

Charles Spurgeon famously said in one of his sermons: "The same sun which melts wax hardens clay. And the same Gospel which melts some persons to repentance hardens others in their sins."[12] I think if Spurgeon were a gardener, he might more have said that the same sun which wilts the poppy blooms the cosmos. Or the same sun which bolts spinach sweetens peppers. Or the same sun which burns lettuce ripens sweet potatoes. Well, you get the idea. I just wonder how much suffering we endure that really is doing a work within us. Curing things, healing things, encouraging blooms, sweetening the final fruit. I suppose we could submit ourselves to the work, or we could let it destroy us. I want to be like a flower but maybe I need to be more like an onion. (Father Capon would understand.[13])

A few years ago, a family friend of ours in our church experienced the unimaginable suffering of giving birth to a stillborn daughter. I remember the day when they returned to church for the first time, and I felt an almost holy awe around them. As if they had brushed the terrifying closeness of God and lived to tell about it. How can one experience such loss and grief and still walk through those doors and greet those in the body? How is it possible? My pastor talked about how they were like a burning bush that was not consumed. That it was only the grace of God that could sustain someone through that kind of suffering in such a powerful way.

Tony Reinke summarized John Newton's views of suffering quite stunningly. My pastor shared this quote in a sermon and I scribbled it down as quickly as I could:

> Some Christians are called to endure a disproportionate amount of suffering. Such Christians are a spectacle of grace to the church, like flaming bushes unconsumed, and cause us to ask, like Moses: "Why is this bush not burned up?" The strength and stability of these believers can be explained only by the miracle of God's sustaining grace. The God who sustains Christians in unceasing pain is the same God—with the same grace—who sustains me in my smaller sufferings. We marvel at God's persevering grace and grow in our confidence in him as he governs our lives.[14]

Burning bushes who are not consumed.
Suffering that does not destroy us.
Heat that melts our hearts.

## Cultivate

Learn how to care for your heat-weary plants. Water them thoroughly before the sun gets high in the sky. Tie up your leaves over your cauliflower to keep them from blanching. Round the hills of the potatoes with more dirt to keep them cool and growing. Give extra water to those who need it.

Have a solid plan for watering your garden. Some gardeners use irrigation hoses or sprinkler systems, while others are content to water with a handheld hose or watering can. No matter what you choose to do, water consistently. The garden needs about one inch of water a week, which doesn't sound like much until you realize it means the entire garden, each square inch, needs that one-inch-deep watering.[15] If you live somewhere where it rains often enough, you might not need to worry about this. However, for most of the United States, gardeners need a plan to water evenly, consistently, and regularly. I often water in the evenings while the sun sets. This is built into my rhythms of summer quiet and peace. Ending the day with a watering hose in my hand feels like peak summer to me. It takes time and patience. We even have a soil moisture meter that tells me how dry the ground is. Usually when I think I have watered enough, a slight dig in the dirt will tell me I haven't even started.

It should be at the top of your list to learn to care for the garden as the summer cooks with its heat.

# 35

# Blood, Sweat, and Tears: The War of the Summer Garden

*If you don't sacrifice for what you want,*
*what you want becomes the sacrifice.*

*Warm red drops* on the earth,
dirt smeared with the blood on my hands.
This is the war of making home again.
Another rose has stuck her thorn.

I cannot strip another layer.
The sweat pours down my back
and off my brow and even when I wipe it away,
I only make a further mess.
Now the blood and sweat have streaked
and I look like a war-ragged soldier.
The dirt I am made of is smeared under my eyes.

## 35 ⚜ Blood, Sweat, and Tears: The War of the Summer Garden

*Oh, how pretty,*
is what the strangers say.
I call them strangers because they must not be gardeners.
And those who garden know.
They see the beds and the dirt,
the tansy with wild yellow tops,
the foxglove heavy-laden with jewels,
the onions towering, the garlic regal and unbent,
the potatoes, the peonies,
the roses, the ground cherries
And they instead ask how my hands are doing.
*How raw are the edges of your palms?*
*How torn are your fingertips?*
*How is that scar where the shears sliced deep and red?*
My best friend sends me a photo of her dirt-stained nail beds.
She, too, has spent her days and nights on her knees,
pulling at the earth, making her hands bleed,
crying when the deer eat her budding roses,
and when the dahlias fail,
as I did when the sweet potato slips arrived two weeks late and dead
and the radishes never plumped
and the David Austin shriveled up over winter.
It feels like every square inch of this dirt has absorbed my blood, my sweat, and my tears.
I have cut myself open, given my heart, invested my strength into this dirt that fights against me.

## Summer

This dirt has seen me weep, scream, curse, laugh, beg, and wait.
It knows the name of every person I love,
every human tragedy I've lived through,
every regret, every hope, every child I've held or dreamed of,
and still it fights me, spade and rock.
I have pushed back the darkness as far as it will go
into the dry and rotten and soggy and fallow.
But those who pass me and see me, shoulders pressing into the ground should not be mistaken:
I do not pray to the earth,
just desperate prayers from the dust that my very soul is made of,
the soil I was made from,
asking for there to be life here
even when the blight hits,
the watermelons never turn pink,
the chickens rip out the small dill sprouts,
the strawberries, just about to ripen.

*Oh, how pretty* is not what I think at all.
*What do you think of this slice of my soul?* I resist asking the stranger.
I just stand in the center alone at golden hour and ask God to remember
my blood, sweat, and tears that cry out from the ground.

## 35 ❦ Blood, Sweat, and Tears: The War of the Summer Garden

### Cultivate

Find beauty in the mess. This is where real life happens, after all. It's not in the perfectly curated social media feeds or the end result of all of the labor. It happens in the hot Saturday afternoons and sliced fingers covered with Band-Aids. The beauty of the earth beneath our nails, the sweat that is poured out, this practice of mirroring our Creator in pushing back chaos and bringing order to these plots of ground.

Make a list of the prayers you've prayed, the messes you've seen, the hardest days of work, and see how the Lord has taught you about himself through those things.

Jesus, the one who has gone before us, knows the labor of blood, sweat, and tears in a garden.

# 36

# Easy Fruit and Abundant Harvests

*Homegrown tomatoes, homegrown tomatoes*
*Wha'd life be without homegrown tomatoes*

*My favorite accidental thing* to do in the summer is to forget about the garden for just a day or two or more. When our days are spent running from friend's house to beach meet-ups, trips to Vermont and drives to camp, it's not that hard to have a break from walking those paths as the morning sun rises. What happens in the garden during the summer when there is no one there to observe it, seems a bewildering mystery. It is why most people garden, to see the culmination of everything colorful and ready to be harvested; from red cayenne peppers and habaneros to fat cucumbers hiding beneath the vines, blushing red tomatoes and stretches of pumpkins and gourds sprawling every which way. Just a few days away will reveal how busy the garden has been in our absence. Sometimes all it takes is one sleep. Like a pile of presents on Christmas morning, summer gardens yield the same wonder. Gifts appear overnight.

The garden is so abundant this time of year that even my kids want to join in the fun. Callan will run to pick any tomato that is even hinting at a pink. Madeleine is eager to see what has changed, and she brings a basket to gather whatever lettuce, herbs, or cucumbers she can find.

We have piles of zucchini in the fridge,
a mountain of tomatoes ripening on the counter,
more than 400 onions curing in the barn,
garlic to tie,
hundreds of potatoes hanging in the basement stairwell,
cabbage and cucumbers and dill fermenting in jars,
curtido fermenting in others,
bright hot peppers sitting in vinegar for hot sauce,
and this is still the middle of harvest season.

Every meal now revolves around the garden. Every jar I can spare has a handful of fresh flowers. Even the kids' rooms will get a splash of cosmos and zinnias every now and then.

This is the kind of season in gardening that makes it possible to forget the hand-cramping work it took to get there. Like a mother after giving birth, the pain becomes a distant memory in light of the beauty gathering up in your arms. It doesn't take much to evoke this joyful reaction from a gardener. I've seen friends post a photo of a singular tomato or handful of peas and their joy is nearly contagious. There's a meme that's making its way around the internet that says something like "I'm so glad I spent months of my life and thousands of dollars for one single vegetable." I have yet to meet a gardener who truly bemoans the work of gardening, even if it does produce only one vegetable. In fact, that one vegetable might be enough to challenge the gardener to try again next year. It's the most wonderful and maddening kind of game to compete against yourself and the cursed ground. The triumph of harvesting is nothing short of a miracle.

"I grew this!" you'll want to shout. You'll find the perfect way to eat it, share it, and enjoy it. You may even find yourself talking about it for days. Just the other day, a friend of mine brought her first tomato to the beach for her lunch. It was the final beach day of the summer and the sun was beating down, heating my pasta salad to a lukewarm, somewhat nauseating temperature. But not for her. She had her lunch planned out: the first tomato sandwich of the summer and she was going to savor every bite.

"Was it as good as you hoped?" I asked as she ate her lunch in some bubble of bliss. She closed her eyes and smiled while she nodded and chewed. The kids were throwing handfuls of sand, the seagulls dove for scattered pretzels and watermelon chunks tossed by the teens, the younger boys ran in circles around our chairs, but she was unfazed. The first tomato of the season from her garden. The first tomato sandwich of the summer. Only a true gardener would understand this moment completely.

So whether you're harvesting one zucchini, a handful of peas, or baskets full of your winter storage vegetables, give thanks. Just as all days and seasons, this too shall pass. For all our labor, every now and then the garden gives up its best to us with ease, abundance, and joy. Eat it up.

## Cultivate

"We must work the works of him who sent me while it is day; night is coming, when no one can work" (John 9:4).

Jesus, you are the Lord of the harvest.
Teach us to enter your fields with open hands and joy as we
    fill your baskets.
May we celebrate over one soul and small harvests
as though we can hear the angels sing over it.
Give us eyes to see the day, hands ready to gather,
and the urgency to work the fields until the last drop of sun
    drops behind the hill.

# 37

# The Days of Light

*Glory be to God for dappled things...*

*T*he *day* is extended.

Another chance to work the fields until the first star flickers above the tree line.

Or is it a firefly? A blinking light of joy as the sun sets in the east.

The dark never rushes in at this time of year,
Night and day linger in the doorway,
Two old friends catching up, saying *Sleep well* and
*See you tomorrow* and *How was the day*,
and *Are you doing alright?*

The day is golden, from that jewel-toned morning light stretching her limbs, all the way to the golden half-light that kisses my children's cheeks and warms the wing of the monarch as she goes from milkweed leaf to milkweed stem, giving her young a place to grow. The light splits through the dandelion puffs, the Queen Anne's Lace, and the tall grass in the field.

It curves around the old trees, ripens the fruit, and sends cotton candy clouds into the twilight as if to give her old friend a midnight snack before she calls it a day.

The day is long, giving us a leisurely dinner hour where the dogs run around as we drink lemonade and push the swing and listen to Bill Withers sing about the lovely day. The molasses-like sunshine gives us more time for the fire, for stories, for running barefoot around the field and the barn a few more times, catching fireflies in a jar, tossing cookies up to the bats as they swoop low, and listening to the cicada song as the world drifts off to sleep.

The daylight is a tumbling ball down the hill, bouncing further than you'd think it will go, somehow reaching its end and going on. "What time is it?" someone asks incredulously. "10:08 p.m.," another replies and it's still light enough to see each other's faces and the sticky residue of s'mores on my son's hands as he climbs into my husband's lap.

The sunflowers still lean toward the west as the golden light drops below the horizon. The soil is still warm. We can still pick honey peas and point out the hidden pumpkins and check for blushing tomatoes before we go inside.

The day arrives early and stays late and I cannot rest.

The sun calls to me as a sage, calling from the window ledge.

## Summer

Wisdom calling in the street telling me it's time to rise.

There is no rest. The garden needs water and overnight the weeds have grown and that handbasket is full of seeds I have yet to sow.

With one post in morning and the other at midnight,

I spend my days swinging and kicking in summer wonder and weariness.

Morning is for the flowers, for the water drops filling the birdbath and scattering in a full shower over the beds.

Midnight is for garlic—cleaning, brushing, tying, and pulling dry garlic stem splinters out of my fingertips.

The remnants of the day are long gone as I sweep up a pile of dried garlic stalks, ready to return in just four hours.

I can already hear her humming in the distance.

These are the days of light, when the sun shines for all those who cannot find their way,

For all those who work the fields, who plant for the harvest, water for the harvest, and reap the harvest.

These are the days of hope and there is still time for more to join in the song of the Sower.

Soon the scythe will swing, the patient arms of the vinedresser will prune for the last time, the threshing floor will be clean, the beds will be empty, the feast will begin and we will never know night again.

*37 ❦ The Days of Light*

## Cultivate

Rise early at the first light of the longest day. Use every ounce of daylight you have to weed, plant, harvest, and prune. Join in the work of the long garden days. These days are not unlimited and it's the best time to redeem those extra hours—in the garden, with your family, your community, and your local church. Watch the golden light at dawn and watch it settle back down at night. Water in the mornings and later at night when it's not hot. Harvest before the sun hits a quarter of the way up in the sky. Water your fall garden. Weed what shouldn't remain. Give thanks for the gift of long days and sun.

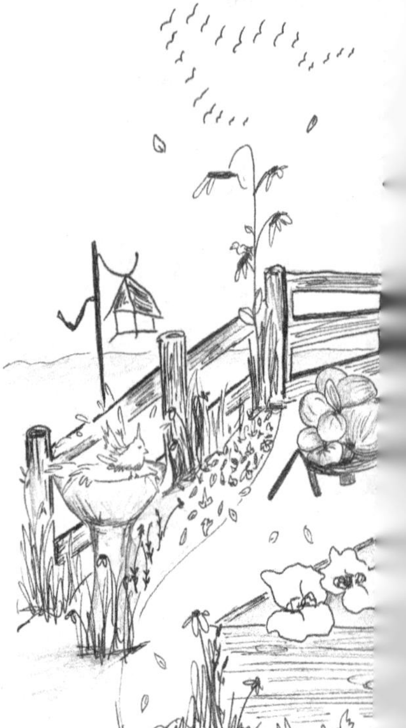

# AUTUMN

# 38

# The Lord of the Harvest

*Sing to the Lord of harvest,*
*Sing songs of love and praise;*
*With joyful hearts and voices*
*Your alleluias raise.*

*By Him the rolling seasons*
*In fruitful order move;*
*O sing to the Lord of harvest,*
*A song of happy love.*

*I once attended a wedding* where the groom nearly stole the show during the processional. As the bride walked down the aisle, his joy overflowed into a rowdy shout and holler that brought all of us to laughter. His voice raised above us in a cheer that announced, "She's here! The one I've been waiting for! There she is!"

The moment took my breath away and brought me to tears. I'm used to emotive grooms whose lips quiver and they cry as their bride walks toward them. But a cheer? A shout? True jubilation and celebration? I could hardly contain my own heart bursting at *his* joy.

*Maybe*, I thought to myself, *maybe I've just witnessed what I can only imagine to be a picture of Christ at the end—albeit dim.* When his church is presented to him, robed in white, and he lets out a joyful, rowdy cheer that lets all of creation know "It's time. Bring the feast, bring the wine, she's here!"

I sense a taste of this as the garden reaches its peak and begins to shout with joy at every harvest, every turned leaf and basketful. A shout of creation, the Lord of the harvest inviting us all to come. It is finished!

And along with this cheerful shout comes the bleak truth that not everything has made it to the end. The garden has become a wild overgrown project, and what remained to the end persevered through the storms, the snows, the drought, the forgotten weeds, and still persisted to bring fruit and joy to our home. The harvest was not wasted. Yet the scraggly and diseased remains will now get raked up, cut back, or piled in the burn pile for our last big fire of the season. The pine branches and brush are lit. My husband watches over the flames with a hose as the smoke announces to all of our neighbors that we are joining in the seasonal expulsion. This is it. The last burn. The scraps of weeds that cannot be composted, dried out sunflower stems—remains of the summer now dead and gone.

Paul writes in 1 Corinthians, "If anyone's work is burned up, he will suffer loss, though he himself will be saved, but only as through fire." I know my life will feel short when it ends and all the work I've done, year after year, at home, at church, in relationships, in this broken world—it will burn up. In a snap of fingers, all of my work and toil will be just branches on the last burn pile. When Christ returns, I pray some of what I did remains to the end. Despite my doubts, my fears, the droughts, the storms—Lord of the harvest, this is my prayer—please let there be something to harvest in the end.

As our last pile burns, the flames lick up the sky and the pine branches that feed the fire are turned to ash, I see my husband tend to the burning edges of the grass with water. There is plenty to feed the heat. Plenty of branches that failed or that gave up the last fruit and died off. But there remains a good husband who tends the fire. A husband who preserves and protects his bride. A husband who shouts in joy, even if all that remains is just this tired body.

Lord, teach us to celebrate with you at the end of all things. Help us to practice our joyful shouts today, even as we bring in the harvest and let the rest go.

## Cultivate

Autumn bonfires are overlooked in my opinion. Consider a harvest bonfire to burn scraps, celebrate the harvest, and clear some beds or shrubs that need to be removed at the end of the season. Remember to burn only the things that have dried out; nothing green should go on the flame. Let this consuming practice remind you of the work that the Lord does for us and in us.

> Father, you are the Lord of the harvest, including the work of saving my soul.
> Keep me from frivolities that waste my time.
> Keep me from fruitlessness that breaks my branches.
> Keep me from coddling disease within my soul that you want to cure.
> Keep me from befriending sin that you want to smoke out.
> Keep me from a life of performance and showiness that results in nothing at the end.
> Help me to pray even as Amy Carmichael once prayed:
>
>> Give me the love that leads the way,
>> The faith that nothing can dismay,
>> The hope no disappointments tire,
>> The passion that will burn like fire;
>> Let me not sink to be a clod;
>> Make me Thy fuel, Flame of God.[16]

## 39

# The Fall Garden

*Toward the end of September the garden looks strained
and distraught and awry, like an old monk who shows
the wear and tear of having resisted temptation a long time.*

*By the end* of July, the garden starts showing off. The sunflowers tower, the corn is fattening up inside its husks; even some pumpkins have started to turn orange. The reality is that, by July 27, we are less than two months away from autumn. The first hard frost won't wait long beyond the first calendar date of autumn, and all of this work will be mostly done.

Yet on this thick and humid day, I am down on my knees planting carrots. I am banking on a good autumn and plenty of time for my fall garden to grow. The brussels sprouts are in six straight rows. The broccoli seeds in three rows. Ten rows of carrots. Four rows of lettuce. One long row of dragon beans along the edge of the cattle panel trellis. One final row of cilantro for the salsa I'll make in October. If the season works out just right, I might still be able to pull some of these carrots from the ground in December just as I did last year. In a week, I will plant a patch of peas and spinach. Maybe toss a few more flowers in to try my luck. This is the fall garden—a faithful planting even in the most exhausting season of growth.

Of course, as it goes, everything in the garden is teaching me something.

If there's anything I've learned about parenting so far is that you're never just parenting for the season you're in. You're parenting the things you didn't address or see last year, the work and joys this year, and planting seeds for the hope of a future harvest. You're never just investing in today. You're never really done.

I see this everywhere. Exhaustion and weariness don't mean that the work is done. Hardly. In fact, when I'm doing dishes at 9 p.m. and I still have garlic to clean and tie up, and a basket of laundry to fold, a teenager to talk with, a deadline for our church's discipleship study, and several dozen unanswered emails, I'm quite aware that my exhaustion doesn't mean the work is finished. We all love to tout rest and relaxation, as if our whole culture doesn't revolve around a constant race to see who can do as little as possible for as long as possible. Hard work in seasons of already hard work has its own pay off too. As wonderful as rest is, sometimes the best invitation is to sweat a little more, work a little harder, get a little more grit under your fingernails.

I want to spend October and November harvesting from the garden, not putting it to bed just yet. And if I want to do that, it

## 39 ❦ The Fall Garden

starts in July. I've told you that the July garden begins in the January heart, but the October garden is dripping through sweat into the July soil. I'm called to be faithful, and I know part of that faithfulness is right here, with two feet in the summer and my eyes on autumn.

What's most remarkable to me is that there are simply plants that do not love the summer. They faint in the heat and would rather bolt and send out seeds than actually produce the thing they were planted to produce. Take cilantro for example—absolutely hates the heat. If you want to lose your cilantro faster than you can say July, plant it in late spring to mature into the heat. And yet, every year, I keep planting cilantro in May and remember sometime in mid-June that unless I want to succession plant all summer long, I'm better off waiting until the fall. I'm also so eager to try and force something on the garden that it's simply not designed to do.

There are certain varieties of lettuce that love the heat. They're called heat-tolerant, if you're shopping for them. Flashy Trout Back is one. Yet there are some that will tower straight up if I'm not paying attention. They reject the heat and every year I think I'll remember this (I don't). You'd think I would remember this in life, too. Both of my children respond better to gentle, reasonable corrections, and yet I still yell. My husband and I communicate best if we sit down and talk, and I still text in anger. Those I minister to at church come to me for grace and truth, and I still have bad days. I force heat on those who wilt under it, forgetting that God designed some to grow into the cold. Surely if he did that for lettuce, he did something similar for humanity. Is it possible I'm trying to carelessly plant cilantro in May everywhere I go in my life?

These are the things I chew on as I plant seed after seed, sweat drenching my forehead and burning my eyes. The work might be more taxing under the summer sun, but the reward is sweeter in the winter cold.

There's also the beautiful truth that the fall garden is only here because something else was harvested. We don't like endings and yet, everything in the garden reminds me that in order for one thing to grow, something else likely has to die, rot, get pulled, or moved. The fall beds are where the garlic was for most of the last eight months. Once the garlic was harvested, these beds were wide open and ready for either rest or a reset. On a smothering hot day, a young woman from church came by to learn about gardening and most of what we did was clear those beds. It didn't seem like much in the way of teaching about gardening, but it was the most honest picture of what most of the work is: raking, pulling, clearing, and piling, on repeat.

This is the work of sanctification, as well. I can see it right here with my hands. Just when you think you've done it, been fruitful and faithful, the harvest comes in, the ground is cleared, and the next work begins. While the garlic grew, the weeds grew. I let them stay, knowing I would deal with them after harvest. It makes me wonder how much of myself the Lord is graciously patient with until he clears the work and begins the next one. Because if I garden like him, he'll get to the bottom of all of those things as soon as the fruit comes into the storehouse.

So I plant in faith, knowing that these beds will be cleared in a matter of months for whatever the next crop or season will be. This sweat will turn to ice, and there will be time to put it all to bed.

But not today.

## Cultivate

Look at your growing season and your garden zone. How many days do you have until your first autumn frost? If you have time, make a plan for a moderate fall or winter garden. See if you can extend your growing season a bit with some cool weather crops, and watch the work of sanctification with your own hands.

Favorite cool weather crops in our garden include carrots, Brussels sprouts, and the kale that returns year after year.

## 40

# The Feasting Season

*At harvest time, even the gardener, with his table
piled and cellar full, eats like a king.*

*G*ive thanks!
For the baskets full,
the jars on the shelves,
the freezer stocked,
the hanging braids,
the petals pressed,
the herbs dried.

Give thanks!
For the bright green lettuce,
the red, pink, blushing tomatoes,
the spicy peppers,
the sweet corn,

the pickles in the jar,
the cucumbers, sliced to delicacy.

Give thanks!
For the herbs stuffed in a chicken roast,
the potatoes and carrots surrounding it,
the onions chopped and garlic minced,
a twisted citrus sparking the air,
the smell of a fruitful life.

Give thanks!
For the bouquets that filled the hallway tables,
and dining room centerpieces,
that were given at hospital visits, birthday parties, weddings, and office desks.
For handfuls of flowers picked by children,
set in small jars on windowsills
until they shriveled into watercolor pastels of what they were.

Give thanks!
For the limes squeezed from the tree,
the lemons sliced, bright yellow and sharp,
for the figs, purple and rich,
for the quince and apples,
plums and peaches,
cherries and berries;
all of the fruits that sit sweet on our lips,
tender gifts of mercy in such a harsh world.

*Autumn*

Give thanks!
For the wheelbarrows full of pumpkins,
the gourds, orange and green,
the squash, long and heavy,
the broom corn brushing the sky,
the sweet corn fattening up with husks.

Give thanks!
For the farmers' fields,
the roadside stands piled high with food,
the CSAs and deliveries and farmer's markets,
the fresh and ripe and spilling goodness,
of the earth that still yields its fruit in season,
despite our battering and pummeling and stripping it all away,
the Lord calls it to provide again and again,
and we sit at the table and feast.

Give thanks for the feasting season.
Fill your table with friends.
Pour the drinks and light the candles.
Set the music low and dance for joy.
in the kitchens and root cellars,
in the winery and barns,
in the greenhouses and fields,
husbands and wives and friends and family,
children and grandparents and neighbors alike,
come into the feast and give thanks for the gift of another year.

Our King has not forgotten us.
Our big Brother has sharpened his scythe.
Our Father has opened up the doors.

"The Spirit and the Bride say, 'Come.'
And let the one who hears say, 'Come.'
And let the one who is thirsty come;
let the one who desires take the water of life without price."

(Revelation 22:17)

## Cultivate

Host a meal to celebrate the harvest and invite neighbors, friends, coworkers, family. Plan a meal around what you grew, no matter how small or big. If you can, use local produce from farm stands and local meat to subsidize and fill in the gaps. Eat a hundred-mile meal and give thanks for the season. Wherever you live, this can be accomplished by knowing local farmers, knowing your own seasons and crop peak seasons, and planning a meal around these things. Perhaps it means the crown of the meal is a dessert with fruit that is only in season once a year. Or maybe an appetizer with that one vegetable that costs an arm and a leg in every other season except right now.

## 41

# Remembering Failures

*If a thing is worth doing, it is worth doing badly.*

*I'm standing in* the middle of my garden rows with that mid-September sun filling the beds. It almost has me fooled that it's mid-July, but the garden knows. She is giving up the last of her summer yield and I'm remembering all of the things I was so excited to plant this year that didn't make it to this day. I know I lean melancholy, but there is always a sense of the garden that *could have been* and the garden *I have*. Whether by lack of knowledge, time, or energy, I couldn't cross that bridge and all of my garden failures seem stacked up in invisible places around the garden that is now nodding its head toward the sleepy autumn.

I imagine there are gardens out there that do not fail. Where the seeds planted always produce, there is never a pest in sight, and never a rodent or storm or neglect that walks the paths. In that garden, everything grows, nothing rots, and all is preserved.

## 41 ❦ Remembering Failures

But that's not where I live. I live in the creation that is still groaning and waiting for redemption. In it, I too groan when I realize that a failed harvest is inevitable for one crop or another. When the luffa never fruits before the frost, when the squash bugs devour the gourds, when the watermelon never quite makes it on the yellowing and dying vine. Or worse yet, there's a small pang of grief when a harvest that I imagined would fill my shelves only provides a handful of what I wanted. I suppose it's not a failure that I only have one cup worth of dried black beans. I just didn't realize I would need to plant five times as many if I wanted enough for seed and for our weekly taco nights. There was one year I couldn't get the dill to grow. I couldn't figure out why, but it just didn't want to live in my garden. There was the year the tomatillos grew their husks but failed to grow to size within the husks. The year all of my broccoli decided to grow tall and green, but never produced one single broccoli head. The garden is just as much a tally of my failures as it is my successes.

However, if you're looking at gardening as a lifelong habit, there's a good chance you'll have many gardens ahead of you to fix what went wrong this year. Or to abandon certain plans altogether. Every failure, I tell myself, is just an opportunity to learn. As corny as this sounds, it's the truth when it comes to the work of the ground. The most I have ever learned came from the broken, diseased, or barren plants that I hold in my hands. These are the things that prompt the questions—What did I do wrong? What can I do differently next time? What did I miss?

Truth be told, remembering failures is the only light in which I can truly see the sanctifying work of God. Because I certainly remember my failures. I remember what not to do again. I can see what I neglected. And I can see how the way out isn't through repetition.

I won't plant the tomatoes that close together again.

I won't turn a blind eye to weeds like that again.

I won't neglect pruning or pinching again.

But also, I won't hide sin like that again.

I won't try to live a life of image-protection again.

I won't try to live a life of isolation from Christian community again.

Isn't this the entirety of Scripture? Look how we failed! And look how God was faithful.

This is the reminder as I walk these beds and look at all of the things that I was unable to do well—a dichotomy of failure and faithfulness. All of the failed crops, failed blooms, failed harvests. And yet, look at all that was good. Failures aren't the final summation of this work, even if failure is all I have to show. Because next year, I am less likely to fail in these things, at least, not in the same way. Next year, the garden will grow differently. This year, the garden grew, I learned, and I failed, and somehow the end is still sweet. This is the common grace of God, right here in these garden paths.

## Cultivate

This is where a garden journal becomes absolutely essential. You will likely forget the minute details of your failures when next season rolls around. Keep track of what didn't work. This is a good habit to establish all season, but if you didn't do that, the end of the season is a good time to walk through your garden and note everything you want to do differently next year. Note the weeds that were the most voracious. Note what you want less or more to harvest. Note what diseases destroyed what crops, what deficiencies you noticed, what pests were the most damaging, and so on. This will be a gentle roadmap for you as you return to gardening next season.

Remember your salvation—where has God redeemed you from your failures? Make notes in your journal of these reminders, too. These shouldn't serve as shame-giving memories but rather places where we have seen God's redeeming hand.

## 42

# Watch the Farmer

*God said, "I need somebody willing to sit up all night with a newborn colt. And watch it die. Then dry his eyes and say, 'Maybe next year.' I need somebody who can shape an ax handle from a persimmon sprout, shoe a horse with a hunk of car tire, who can make harness out of haywire, feed sacks and shoe scraps. And who, planting time and harvest season, will finish his forty-hour week by Tuesday noon, then, pain'n from 'tractor back,' put in another seventy-two hours." So God made a farmer.*

*I've learned to* watch the farmer:

How the tractors pull along deep ruts, familiar and fertile.

How the corn falls, how the pumpkins grow, how the lights stay on in the barn after dusk.

I've learned to listen to the way they talk about the land, the animals, the harvest.

## 42 · Watch the Farmer

The farmer who stops by to drop off meat from the butcher and tosses marrow-filled bones to my dogs and tells me of the perfect cow for beef.

The old Christmas tree farmer on Harris Road who pauses our conversation to dig out a honeynut squash and tells me to cook it for dinner and let him know what I think.

The farmer who tells me about the organic matter that his pumpkins love.

The farmer up the road who has perfected his own variety of apple named after his grandmother Scarlet.

I watch for when the farmer harvests, for when they fill their barns.

And I watch for the day when they shut down the farm stands, hanging hand-painted "Closed" and "See You Next Season" signs sideways over empty shelves at the end of driveways.

I've learned to notice when the farm fields go up for sale, dug out deep with new foundations and developments with names like "Grandview Estates."

Houses built where hearts once poured their lives out, on that same fertile ground.

I remember the farmstead down the road in my childhood and the stories of the estate, the bitter woman who stole it from him, how she let the homestead fall into disrepair, and the old farmer who would sit across the valley in his truck, day after day, watching the place that housed generations slowly rot back into the ground.

I remember my childhood pastor with a farm heritage, who could talk about dairy and planting seasons, a whole Sunday sermon on agriculture, who tried to plant some seeds in the hearts of country folk on hill in a tiny church in a forgettable town.

I am one of them.

I've watched the farmers all my life. The ones I went to school with, the ones who wouldn't be in class for weeks because it was planting season or harvest season or calving season.

The friends who ran off to FFA and 4H and showed at the county fair and maybe understood something at fifteen that I wouldn't learn for another twenty years.

Watch the farmer—when he plants, when he worries, when he stands in his fields with his hat in his hand, when he turns the apple on the tree and looks under the leaves, when he waters, when he fertilizes, when he rises, and when he sleeps.

Watch the farmer—when the family goes to the field, and the farmer's wife is delivering dinner by four-wheeler, and the farm-stand opens early, and closes too soon. Watch the farmer when the frost kills a harvest, when blight strikes, when an invasive pest eats away half of their orchard.

Watch the farmer—they have learned how to set the pace of their feet and hands to the pace of the seasons, to the pace of a world that will inevitably disappoint. They rise and fall with the song that rises from an empty field, a barren field, a tired field. And they know the difference between these things.

Watch the farmer—does he not toil and sweat? Does he not watch over every season, every movement, every moment with eyes toward the harvest? Does not our Father care for the fields even more?

## Cultivate

Know your local farmer. There will inevitably be things you cannot grow as prolifically as the local farmer can. Be a regular at the farmstand, ask questions, listen, and learn. Support the local work of generational farming. Source your meals, your meat, your vegetables, your cheese, whatever it may be from the farm itself. Get a little more comfortable with the smell of manure and the muddy fields that keep this world fed. Support the new, young, and eager farms that want to return a love of agriculture to our dining rooms. Support u-pick and farm-to-table dinners and honor the men and women who never gave up on the ground. Go to your county fair and applaud the kid who is showing his prized sow, her blue-ribbon pumpkin. Buy the fruit pies from the farmer's wife, learn to eat in season, and become a fan of the steady work of farmers.

# 43

# Good Soil

*A garden is only as good as the soil it grows in.*

*T**he one thing* it seems most people forget about when it comes to their backyard potagers, potted plants, garden patches, or market long beds is that the soil is a major component of the health of your garden. In fact, it's not just a major component—it is what will make or break your entire garden experience. It doesn't matter how good your seed stock is, how much energy you have, how fervent you intend to be with fertilizers and pesticides. If your soil isn't healthy, your garden will suffer. Picture the old farmer bending low to the dirt, picking up a handful in his hands, letting the wind blow through it as he watches the clumps fall back down. This is the first thing that matters. The dirt.

When we first bought our property in 2017, we tested our soil to see what the nutrient needs were in the empty field. A small vial of soil was all we needed. We were able to purchase a fairly reliable

## 43 · Good Soil

soil testing kit online, though some local government offices offer this as well. Already we knew that the soil tended toward clay, and it was rock solid underneath the grass. It was going to need a lot of work to get the soil ready for planting.

Our nutrient test revealed that our soil was completely depleted from all nutrients. A kitchen without food. A canvas without paint. Nothing to work with. Nitrogen, phosphorus, potassium—without these, a garden will whimper and wilt. That year, we tilled the ground, broke up the clay, and did what we could to feed it. I joked that year that I had a magical "hobbit" touch to grow miniature vegetables because everything we grew only developed to about half of its size. It was comical at best, but we did what we could with the soil we had. The next year, I had a jug of fish fertilizer that I made sure to add to every bed. It was disgusting and I had flashbacks to fourth-grade field trips to the Iroquois Indian Museum, learning about how they would bury dead fish in their garden beds. I should have realized then that I had a lot to learn from those ancient ways and the smell of decaying fish was just the start of it. So I'd dilute the dark fluid, water all of the beds, and watch as the hard and forgotten soil slowly gave in to a more loamy, black, rich dirt.

By the third year, we were adding our own compost and leaf mulch to the beds, along with chicken manure at the end of the growing season. We eventually transitioned most of our garden beds to no-till beds, meaning we're adding compost to them year after year but have no more need for those awkward tillers, removing the sod, or broadforks. Year by year, the soil has improved since then and, year by year, the garden fruit has reflected it. (I even grow full-size vegetables now!) Most of the time, a problem we have in the garden can be directly pointed back to the soil underneath it. A healthy foundation is more important than all of the trellises, pest deterrents, and planting styles combined. Isaiah 7:9b says,

> If you are not firm in faith,
> you will not be firm at all.

This replays in my head as I'm thinking about our garden, what end of season improvements are needed, and the work I have to do to get there. Good soil is good soil. It's not debatable. You'd be hard pressed to find a gardener who wants to plant his crops in hard, clay ground. Fallow ground is a part of the process, but it's not plantable. It needs care. It needs to be healthy again. If we're not firm in our faith, we will not be firm at all. If we're not planted in good soil, what good is it, really? If we're not living our lives from a place of truth, a place where God is tending to us, where we're growing and learning—we're not going to be truly alive at all. We'll be one season away from fallow. One season away from disease. One season away from root rot, nutrient-stripped land, and fruitlessness.

The Parable of the Sower in Matthew 13 might as well be called the parable of the soil. Jesus even gives us examples of the poor ground—exposed and vulnerable soil on the path, rocky soil, shallow soil, weed-ridden soil, and finally good soil. The seed was good in every place it was sown; it was the soil that made all of the difference. We spend so many of our days trying to make our lives look good. We polish the surface of our image, carefully managing whatever we think is overgrown or not impressive. We'll brag about our fruit, the things we produce. Even with good intentions, we tend to the visible stuff first. We fool ourselves into thinking the hidden stuff will stay hidden and can just be handled later, when we're more mature, when we have more time, when we can get around to it.

But bad soil will always reveal itself. It shows in the half-sized corn cobs, the diseased leaves, the pests that slept beneath the surface and now feed on what could have been good. I do wonder how much healthier my own life would be if I spent more time tending the soil that is nurturing my heart. If I'm not firm in faith, I'm not firm at all. And no one will be left wondering; the things that are hidden do not stay hidden forever.

## Cultivate

If you have a yard covered with leaves, consider gathering them up to cover your garden beds for the winter or any new beds you'll want to plant in the spring. The autumn leaves serve more of a purpose than just beauty. They can add health right back to your soil, compost bins, or mulched pathways. One website recommends shredding them or mowing them over several times to get them to the consistency you'd want in the beds.[17] We've used leaves to cover the sod on new spaces so that in the spring, it's a much easier job to add compost or soil for planting. Cover crops are another thing to consider for fall planting. A little internet sleuthing will help you find the best cover crop to plant on a bed that needs nutrient restoration or seasonal rest. Common cover crops include rye, clover, mustard, and hairy vetch.

> Sow for yourselves righteousness;
> > reap steadfast love;
> > break up your fallow ground,
> for it is the time to seek the LORD,
> > that he may come and rain righteousness upon you.
>
> (Hosea 10:12)

Find some fallow ground, an empty field, and pray this:

> Father, would you break up the fallow ground within me,
> the soil that I have never nourished, but depleted,
> growing my own pleasures,
> my own idols,
> my own meager harvest of dust,
> and emptying the ground of every last good thing it had.
>
> Where there was joy, I squandered it.
> Where there was faith, I've forgotten it.
> Where there was kindness, I faked it.
> Where there was gentleness, I kicked it.
> Where there was goodness, I planted cynicism.
> Where there was patience, I planted hurry.
> Where there was self-control, I planted more of me.

## 43 ⚜ Good Soil

Where there was faithfulness, I planted less of you.
Where there was peace, I wasted it.
Where there was hope, I pulled it.
Where there was contentment, I spit on it.
Where there was provision, I dug for more.
Where there was love, I suffocated it,
and even the rocks do not cry out as they fill the corners of
my heart.

Father, sow righteousness in me.
Soften me by your Spirit.
Break up the ground.
Your blood the only thing to
fertilize,
soften,
water,
restore.
Your body the only thing to
humble,
remind,
discomfort,
unearth.
And help me to kneel here again,
to seek you at the place where
you have broken me.
Lord, bring the rain.

## 44

# Preparing for Death

*[The black frost] drops down like a curtain between the show of the garden and the audience of the house. The play is over; our thoughts turn indoorward. Night and the rain wrap round comfortably like an old coat.*

*These days are* the final days. A black swallowtail butterfly that I watched grow as a caterpillar and curl into the pre-chrysalis curve on my dill now dips with its black and blue painted wings around the decaying flowers and drying out beds. This actually brings me to tears. This petal-in-flight creature bounces from rudbeckia stem to the nasturtium and back to the dill, almost as if to say again, another echoing, "Thank you! We made it!" Another summer of growing and nurturing life, and now it passes away behind me, bouncing along the fading sunlight. The garden is its own factory of goodbyes, farewells, and thank yous.

In his 1929 book *The Gardener's Bed Book*, Richardson Wright writes about how, once the katydids start humming, you can start counting down the days until the first hard frost of the year. The other night, Madeleine and I stood under the lilac tree and heard the katydids rattle, and noted the date. The frost is coming. Gather up what you can. All of creation groans. As we look toward the fall and the last home stretch, it's hard for me to not wonder if any of this mattered. That familiar melancholy rises up in me—was all of this work worth it?

The groaning sigh of my children when I asked them to help me weed or harvest.

The blistering rashes from whatever poisonous plant was growing in between my onions.

The edamame that we waited all season for that only produced enough for one or two meals.

The sweat of my husband as he buried the deer fencing and stapled it up six feet high, just to make sure the garden was protected.

The swinging of his scythe in the field to have hay to toss in the chicken coop.

Every small little and forgettable effort—was it worth it? Will we get to do it again? Will anyone who comes after me even remember the girl who tried to carry on some kind of legacy through dirt and seeds?

When I was seventeen, I went to Ireland for the first time with my mother. We stayed in a bed and breakfast just west of Cork with an old farmer and his wife. Upon sight of their piano, I sat down to plunk out a few tunes. Once Mr. O'Sullivan realized I was a musician, he came right over and we spent a good part of that evening singing old Irish standards. He had a beautiful tenor voice and smelled like the earth and tea. It was a memorable night for me. Nearly twenty years later, I went back again to Ireland with my mom and my sister. We thought we'd take a chance and try to find the same bed and breakfast again. Sure enough, the farmhouse B&B was still running and my mother booked a night. As I was pulling my suitcase up the front sidewalk, the front door swung open and there was the farmer's wife, Mrs. O'Sullivan.

"It's you!" she gasped. I laughed, unsure if she actually knew who or what she was talking about. It had been twenty years. Surely I was not the most memorable person she had met. I greeted her and she started in on her memory.

"You sang with us," she said. "With my husband, at that piano," she gestured to the same old piano in the center of the room. I couldn't believe it. What are the chances? She told me how they remembered that night fondly for years and how special it was to have someone among them who could play and knew all of the old tunes. Naturally, I asked where her husband was.

"He passed away just a few years ago," she said. Within the span of an hour or so, she had the whole evening planned. Her daughter and grandchildren were going to come down from their farm up the hill, and we'd play music for hours until it was time for everyone to go to bed. We even played the song that she said her late husband would sing in the garden as he puttered about day after day.

I tell this story now every time we play Irish music at different pubs and events. This small legacy of a farmer, his piano, an American girl, and the way time holds us all together somehow.

Wendell Berry famously wrote in his poem "Manifesto: The Mad Farmer Liberation Front": *Plant sequoias.*

I take this to mean—plant things that will outlive you. Plant things like legacies, good soil, music that goes from grandfather to grandchild and across the pond and back. Plant seeds even though we have no promise of tomorrow. Plant a garden and know you will not outlive the tended and wild creation; at least not in this life. Live the kind of humble life of that old Irish farmer who I can still picture today and whose memory is now a part of my story too.

What we do will live on in one way or another. The work I did this year will feed the soil and the ground is healthier because I poured my heart into it this season. The birds are still alive and kept singing, the monarchs and swallowtails had a place to hatch among the milkweed and dill, and I like to think these very small things matter. Like a song played on an old piano in the middle of a dim living room somewhere in the south of Ireland. This humble thing of planting a garden, feeding the family, adding to the beauty, it all lingers on somehow. Whether that's through the memories, the cumulative effect of someone caring for the land, or through my children shadowing me as I pick the North Georgia Candy Roaster and they cradle it like a newborn baby in their arms.

This year's garden is coming to a close. The perennials should be cut back or covered with hay, the beds should be mulched, covered with compost, or left to rest completely. We do not have to fear death—not as people of the kingdom. Jesus himself went before us and resurrected in the garden.

Each year, I prepare for the final harvest, the first hard frost that turns everything black and brown, the first ice and freeze. We know it's coming and watch the weather app as the night temperatures drop lower and lower for longer and longer. The air conditioning is turned off and we all see how long we can last before someone turns on the heat. The wind begins to change, that familiar howl around the house eaves, kicking up the leaves. The maple and walnut trees drop a blanket of copper and gold, and heavy walnuts fill our baskets. I daily keep an eye on the temperatures and the remaining fall crops that are still fighting to grow. The sweetest brussels and carrots and a few herbs that remain.

I don't know what this winter holds for us. I don't know how many gardens I have left. Perhaps it's fifty more. Maybe it's none. But I'm going to keep planting sequoias, singing songs with the old farmers, and working the ground until the Lord calls me home.

The katydids are singing; it's time to get ready for bed.

## Cultivate

Get your garden journal ready. Take a note of the first hard frost. This is when the temperatures at night stay below freezing for several hours. This is likely the first "killing" frost. Note what, if anything, still remains that you could harvest or gather—seeds, herbs, dried out flowers for displaying. If you have time before the frost hits, harvest as much as you can. Use up the last of the green tomatoes. Ferment some peppers. Make one final autumn bouquet. Once the frost hits, it's nearly over.

Spend time before the Lord asking what it means to leave a legacy for your life. When the final decay begins, what do you want to remain? Will your life be one of a final burst of abundance and provision for those who come after you? Those plans start now.

## 45

# Preserving for Later

*To be sure, food keeps us alive, but that is only its smallest and most temporary work. Its eternal purpose is to furnish our sensibilities against the day when we shall sit down at the heavenly banquet and see how gracious the Lord is. Nourishment is necessary only for a while; what we shall need forever is taste.*

*I have a running tally* on the side of my refrigerator of everything I've grown, stored, preserved, or canned. I do this partially as a sign of triumph to myself to see everything we accomplished in the garden this year. I also do it because I always forget what I actually put up and find myself searching the freezer and pantry for things I'm certain I had but never actually wrote down.

Seven bags of spinach from May in the freezer. Twelve bags of frozen tomatoes waiting for me to make sauce. Cayenne peppers and habaneros. Lavender-infused oils. Echinacea tinctures. Spreads and salsas, roasted corn, dried herbs, carrot cake jam and raspberry

## 45 ⁕ Preserving for Later

lime jelly, and the list goes on and on. Part of the joy of gardening is actually right now—when everything is sitting on my counter and I'm scrambling for ideas and recipes for how I'll use it all. Two jars of dill sauerkraut sit fermenting on my counter as I type this. Hundreds of tomatoes have ripened next to the reddening peppers and piles of cucumbers. All of our meals revolve around whatever is coming out of the garden right now. I think we manage to eat tomatoes at every single dinner throughout the months of August and September.

If you don't already have one, invest in a large canning pot or a pressure canner. Or both! Canning is a great way to preserve the harvest in ways you can enjoy year-round. Nothing beats opening your own can of tomato sauce or soup in the dead of winter, knowing that it's still the garden living on at your table. I maintain that *Ball* recipes are still the best for most things. There are certain areas you can take a bit more liberty in, such as salsas and pickling, while in others you need to abide by the rules strictly to avoid disease (botulism is bad.) Pick up a *Ball* canning cookbook or scour the internet for good recipes. Jams and jellies can be made year-round as well. I've saved my raspberries for a cool fall day when I won't mind steam filling my kitchen for a round of jam-making. Depending on what you want to eat and enjoy eating, now is the time to really preserve the fresh stuff before it goes bad.

This year, we made our own hot pepper sauce. It's our own Burke brand of whatever hot sauce you toss on wings or pizza. It sat in a brine for about a week before I added apple cider vinegar, and now it's reached absolute perfection. Unfortunately, I only had enough peppers that time to make one jar. A new pile of habaneros is stacking up as I type for round two.

If you eat a lot of pasta or pizza in the winter, make your own plain tomato-sauce base and put jars up for your winter stock.

Soups and stews? Freeze your carrots, celery, small onions, leeks, and so on to add to butter and sauté on a cold autumn night. I have a friend who gave me the brilliant idea to put all of my greens such as kale in the food processor and freeze the small pieces. The greens look like herbs and spices in chicken noodle soup, and no one is the wiser.

Does your home go through peanut butter and jelly sandwiches? Or morning toast with jam? How about a Thanksgiving cheesecake with homemade preserves spread on the top? You really cannot go wrong with a shelf full of any fruit preserves.

Pickled beans, cucumbers, peppers, fermented cabbage—all of these things make their way onto our burgers, tacos, charcuterie boards, and more throughout the long and dull winters. This year I'm even soaking some cherries from the local farmstand in orange liqueur and cognac, and ginger liqueur and vodka to use as sauces for desserts and entertaining over the holidays.

To keep your herbs, simply cut what you'd like and tie the end with twine. Hang this bunch somewhere out of direct sunlight and let it dry. Grab and crunch a handful of whatever you'd like when the time comes: some crushed thyme over a sizzling steak in the

## 45 ⁂ *Preserving for Later*

pan with butter, sage tossed in a chicken roast, or oregano in the sauce that you put up from your own tomatoes. We also freeze our basil in single layers on parchment paper and then bag them up to keep in the kitchen freezer on hand. This allows me to toss Italian basil into a pasta dish or Thai basil into a chicken and noodle dish, and they're almost as good as fresh.

Lavender sits infusing in almond oil in a jar in my cabinet. I will use this oil to make a hand or skin salve for our dry hands or even next summer's sunburned backs.

Nasturtium flowers, which are jam-packed with Vitamin C, sit infusing in apple cider vinegar along with garlic, hot peppers, and ginger. This concoction will sit for months, with the occasional shake from me, and we'll drink this mixed with honey when anyone comes down sick. My kids dread it, but it's become something of a winter ritual, a way of boosting and helping out our sunshine-depleted immune systems and kick things into high gear. I just highly recommend having something on hand to wash it down as it can be quite ... pungent.

The reality is that preserving is hard and tedious work, but if you can see past the strain to the meal you'll serve or the skin cream you'll give someone at Christmas or the health-boosting tinctures you can enjoy in the dead of winter, you will begin to understand that the garden isn't just about consuming. It's something we carry with us long after the last flower has bloomed.

We live in such a demanding and immediate society. If we want it, we go buy it. This is certainly a luxury that not everyone can afford, and history hasn't always allowed for such convenience either, but this fast and easy consumerism has actually made it really difficult for us to understand why gardens matter.

It wasn't until Covid hit that the world at large started to yearn for something beyond the grocery store. Gardening returned in force. Seeds were selling out. Soil was backordered from the local delivery service. Something in us realized that what we craved wasn't more speed or more convenience; it was something that we had forgotten about entirely.

Gardening isn't just for the elderly who poke around in quiet garden beds. It's for the single mother who feels her grocery budget is stretched too thin. It's for the family who wants to work hard together and celebrate the joys of the harvest in real time. It's for the bachelor who wants to perfect his chef skills and grow all of his own ingredients. It's for the creatives, the dreamers, the hard workers, the taste-testers, the ones who love this earth that God has given us, the people who love the way a fresh cucumber snaps and want to experience that same crunch from a pickle in February. It's for all of us. Gardening is not for the elite or the wealthy, and it's not just for the people who aren't afraid of hard work and working hard. It's for you, our kids, and the earth. In gardening we join the song that all of creation sings, and we join the table set for us in the presence of our enemies. It's the beginning echoes of the wedding feast. I hear it when I pop open a jar of strawberry jam, fresh from the harvest season—the hints of the bells ringing, "It is finished! It is finished! It is finished!"

## 45 ❦ Preserving for Later

### Cultivate

Make a list of all you preserved or saved this year. Whether it's a few bundles of herbs in some jars, or a root cellar full of canned goods and orange squashes, post a list of all you've saved and hope to use before next season. It's easy to slip into a fast-food mindset in the way we cook, looking for what's easy and quick instead of what's in season or in storage. Try to arrange a few recipes around what you have preserved and saved. Recipes go up a notch when you start getting creative with the flavors that are tucked around your kitchen. Things like steak improve greatly with crushed herbs in the pan. Serve compound butter with herbs and garlic blended in. Use jams on different meat or sandwiches throughout the winter. (They aren't obligated to the peanut butter and jelly regime for life!) Use kale in a soup instead of other greens, blended down into small bits in a food processor. Get creative and use what you've stored and grown, and take note of what you don't use by the time spring arrives next year. This should help determine your planting list and preserving plans.

If you enjoy outdoor adventures, you might be familiar with The History Channel's gritty survivalist show *Alone*. In Season 3, contestant Dave Nessia stored up more than thirty fish to eat over time for his meals. However, his concern in not eating them all too quickly resulted in him not eating enough, and he was pulled from the show on day seventy-three for malnutrition and having lost too much weight. He had the food he needed right there but chose not to eat it out of fear and a heightened sense of planning.

This story comes up frequently when I find myself not wanting to use the tomatoes we canned, the jams, the salsas, whatever it may be.

"Eat the fish," my husband will say, a subtle reminder that storing up for someday but not letting that "someday" actually arrive might be the worst plan of all.

# 46

# Tired and Weary Season

*The coolness of this world grows upon me.*
*It is time to go in and light a wood-fire on the hearth.*

*I have surrendered.* The weeds which I fought so hard against continue to grow, continue to dominate, and I no longer have dominion over them. At this point, I give up. The onion bed which I cleared a month ago is now covered with crabgrass and other various weeds. Every time I came out here, I would say the same thing.

"Oh, I have to weed that bed and clear it."

But did I? No. Did I at least plant a cover or fall crop on the empty beds? Also no.

The tomatoes that didn't ripen have just days left before that first frost hits. Some lay rotten on the ground, either victims of blossom end rot or the rabbits that hop through these paths. Even the harvest will not all make it to the end. I could scrounge up recipes for fried green tomatoes and other salsas, but in all reality, I am tired of things that I have invested in that never seemed to finish their work. They ran out of time. The clock is ticking down to the final seconds and I cannot windowsill-force their ripening at this point. The end has come, and it means leaving the remaining fattening green crop behind.

I forgot to harvest all of the edamame; once again, surrendering to the chaos that overtakes the late-season garden. The sunflowers hang their heads like sad emo teenagers, and I admit the same tired defeat. For all of my efforts to bring order to chaos, and push back darkness in this small corner of earth, creation is still teeming with madness and waiting for redemption. It still desires to overtake and consume all things.

Sometime in September, I raise my white flag. We have done the work. We harvested as much as we could. The flowers have started to fade and the vegetables are starting to rot. It's time to let the chickens in and salvage what we could not.

Every single gardener I know reaches this point. Some sooner than others. Yet as fall looms on the horizon, I feel the pressure of life returning to some less wild and carefree rhythms. I cannot simply lollygag my way through the garden. There are meetings and conference calls, school schedules and play practices. The sun rises later and sets earlier, adding to that encroaching feeling that time is running out. And we are just human. We are limited and bound to our own energy levels and disciplines. At some point, I can sense the garden begin to move away from me, drifting into the sea of chaos and the best I can do is let it go.

These subtle changes begin when I think "I cannot possibly eat one more zucchini" or "I wonder if I leave those potatoes in the ground if they'll come back next year." It's the look across the yard at the garden but never actually going to the gate. It's the sigh at the pile of vegetables on my counter that still need to be processed. I start to feel more and more like Bilbo Baggins—"I feel all thin, sort of *stretched*, if you know what I mean: like butter that has been scraped over too much bread."[18]

There is an old Irish saying that goes "It's not a delay to stop and sharpen the scythe." Rest can often feel like the opposite of getting things done, when in reality, it's the best way to sharpen the scythe. We cannot work if we are too weary to lift our heads. I have told you one of our family mottos is "Go to bed tired," and I feel like I have and will at this point. I am exhausted. Ready for everything to go to sleep.

## Cultivate

Did you know that some plants might aid in the onset of sleep? (For the record, this is not medical advice, just a simple, gardening girl who likes her tea.) I can't help but believe the Lord knew we would be a tense, anxious people when he gave us things like chamomile, valerian, and lavender.

A medical report titled "Chamomile: An herbal medicine of the past with bright future" states: "Traditionally, chamomile preparations such as tea and essential oil aromatherapy have been used to treat insomnia and to induce sedation (calming effects). Chamomile is widely regarded as a mild tranquillizer and sleep-inducer."[19] Here, in these small white and yellow flowers that grow in my garden bed edges and smell sweet like honey, God has given us a gentle nudge. These small blooms dry flat in baskets alongside the hanging lavender in my kitchen, which also has sleep-inducing benefits, a continual reminder that the work of the garden isn't just for the sweaty days and long harvest seasons. It's also for rest.

Our Father gives us bread and drink, just like Elijah in 1 Kings 19, and herbs and tea, and we can find some restoration in seasons of exhaustion through true, restorative rest. Push against the Western mindset of anti-rest. Not all rest is laziness. Some of it is ordained. Nurture healthy rhythms of rest in both your gardening and spiritual life.

> It is in vain that you rise up early
>     and go late to rest,
> eating the bread of anxious toil;
>     for he gives to his beloved sleep. (Psalm 127:2)

47

# Gathering Seeds and Planting for Spring

*What is good is difficult, and what is difficult is rare.*

*If I really* want to keep my children occupied in the autumn, a quick way is to send them to collect seed pods. Callan loves gathering the balloon-like pods of Love-in-a-Puff (also known as heartseed or balloon vine). Occasionally he just loves popping them to find the heart-stamped seeds on the inside. Madeleine loves the milkweed—the way the silk softens in her hands and flies away on the wind. I handle the annoying ones like hollyhock because the casing sticks and irritates my fingers.

I gather whatever dried heads are still on the stems. Those who are actual professionals in this field recommend gathering seeds as close to the natural distribution as possible. Wait until they're nearing maturity on the plant itself before cutting them and bringing them indoors. Once they're nearly there (or even somewhat past due), I'll gather what I can and leave them for the winter days when I'll have time to sort and label.

Some seeds I'll leave—always the sunflowers. The birds will feast on fat sunflower heads long into the cold months and their enthusiasm will result in hundreds of sunflower volunteers in the spring. It's so predictable that I don't even plant sunflowers anymore. I just give a hearty "thank you" in May and move all of the volunteers to where I'd actually like them.

If you planted heirloom seeds, gather what you can. If you're keeping heirloom seeds from vegetables that you're also eating, this part can get a little more difficult but not impossible. The larger the seed, the easier to save. Pumpkins, gourds, and squash are easy end-of-season seed saving projects for the helping hands in your world. Put friends and neighbors and kids to work cleaning them off and laying them all flat to dry until you can pack them away for the spring. Tomatoes, cucumbers, peppers—these take more time and care, but the end goal is the same—dry seeds that aren't covered with vegetable material and don't get moldy. Seeds need to reach maturity before they'll produce. There's nothing useful about an immature seed; it's simply a wasted thing. Have patience, wait for maturity, and then collect as much as you desire. Have a place to store seeds in the dark all winter.

And as we gather seeds, the ironic part is that we're also planting seeds. Seeds in the form of bulbs. Tulips, daffodils, hyacinth, allium—so many flowers that will greet us at the dawn of spring need to go in now. The famous British gardener Monty Don says the secret to the most natural bulb garden is to toss the bulbs on the ground and plant where they land.[20] This will give the most natural appearance, and since that's usually what most of my gardening looks like, that's the strategy I use. Of course, I know others who do it the opposite way, practically measuring the distance between bulbs as they lay them out. Is there a wrong way to plant bulbs? Yes. Not planting them at all.

Honestly, by the time October rolls around, the last thing I'm trying to do is to get back on my knees and dig. I begin to lose my love for the dirt. It feels demanding and somewhat less inspiring to plant something that I know won't show for another six or seven months. And that's if a hungry squirrel or mole doesn't run off with a beloved Miranda Red Double Tulip.

I'm a grumpy gardener when I'm tired. This is the mood this somewhat mild October day finds me in. I'm standing in front of our weed-ridden garden beds that surround our house wondering how I ever managed to get a book deal about gardening. No garden is perfect, however, and one look at the beds around my house will remind you of this. And this is the truth—no matter how many seeds I gather, how many bulbs I scatter, how many perennials I buy—the wild and wily nature of creation will always be pushing back against me. This is the work that calls back to Eden.

*Subdue.*

*Take dominion.*

*Cursed ground.*
*Thorns and thistles.*
*Sweat.*
*And to dust we will return.*

I cannot stop winter by planting a single tulip bulb. Harvesting all of the seeds doesn't guarantee a crop next year. The darkness is encroaching and all of my work, sweat, and grit cannot stop it. If I were to stop gardening and never work this ground again, and we were to move out of this house and leave it to the hands of creation, within a matter of years the earth would claim it back as its own. Creation would devour it. No bulb, no flower, no squash would grow. Just chaos.

So I sigh, one frustrating last look at the work I still have to do and I crawl back on my knees to push back the darkness again. With a small trowel in hand and a bag of bulbs to scatter, I'm asking the Lord to sustain me just another afternoon out here. One more small gesture to say, "God has dominion over you. God has dominion over me. Darkness will not reign forever."

## Cultivate

Plant bulbs! If you cannot plant them outside, plant some in pots and bring them indoors. Nothing dresses up a dismal gray winter day like the green surprise of an eager sprouting bulb. There are so many good websites online to purchase all kinds of bulbs, but make sure you purchase fall-planting bulbs if you're planting outside. Check your zone again to ensure you don't plant something

## 47 ❦ Gathering Seeds and Planting for Spring

that cannot survive your coldest temperatures, or warmest winter days. You want them to stay dormant until it's time for them to grow.

As we do the work of pushing back the darkness of earth for beauty, perhaps this is a good time to reflect and see where you're doing this in your day-to-day life. Volunteer to plant a bulb garden at your church or a local nursing home. Gather seeds and give them away at Christmastime in hopes of spreading the joy of planting to others.

# 48

# Perennial Care for Next Year

*What I need most of all are flowers, always, always.*

*If you haven't* filled any part of your property with perennials, let me tell you know, you are missing out. But prepare yourself for a learning curve.

The first time I ever visited a garden that absolutely took my breath away, it was Olana. Olana is a historical house and state park which wasn't too far from where I grew up. It was owned by Frederic Edwin Church, a famous landscape painter in the Hudson Valley. After visiting his house, I decided it was no wonder he created what he did. The views, the grounds, the house—all stunning. For several summers in a row, my sister would bring me to Olana and the first time we visited, we walked among the gardens and each flower and blooming bush just took my breath away. She was the one who really instilled a love for beautiful and heritage-rich gardens in me. We'd walk the paths and she told me about Tasha Tudor, and I remember writing in my memory "love lies bleeding" as a flower I would grow someday. (To my joy, I now grow it annually.) But the roses, the hollyhock, the salvia, delphinium, echinacea, you name it—it thrived and grew like a painting right there to touch.

The next garden that evoked the same response in me was in Connemara, Ireland, at the Kylemore Abbey. The garden spans nearly six acres and with each turn in the path, I felt my heart want to scream with joy, which I will tell you is not widely acceptable in a *garden* at a *convent*. So I squealed as quietly as I could and took A LOT of pictures. Once again, I was struck with the perennial glory. To my surprise, fuchsia grows wild in Ireland and simply climbed through the brush along the paths like a weed I'd pull at home. If fuchsia grew wild, what other wonders would I find in the perennial paths? A lot. I'll just sum it up there.

I have visited many friends' gardens here locally who grow the most beautiful perennial gardens. Their care to the space, structure, height, color, is beyond anything I fully understand. In fact, the closest comparison I can give you is I feel somewhat akin to how Eve must have felt in the garden when they come and view my gardens—absolute shame. Nakedness. Exposed. A garden is simply not a garden without some area that is hosting a home of perennial plants. I would argue that most Americans have neglected the joy and beauty and ease of mature perennials plants and have instead committed to spending the majority of their Saturday mornings mowing grass. Grass! Is that really the best we can do? It's so exposed and empty.

My friend Ashley has what she lovingly calls her oval garden. I call it the garden of jealousy because every time I visit, I find myself saying "I want that. What's that? I want that, too. Can I take some of that when you split it? I want it." (As you can imagine, this makes her want to have me over all the time.)

She is a flower farmer and one of the best I have ever seen. Her roses unfold into different shades and layers of beauty, her oval garden blooms in succession in such a way that it's never bare, and all around her home, there is a constant show of color and hardy greens. Hydrangea, echinacea, obedient, tulips, hyacinth, daffodils, roses, delphinium, and on I could go. Perennial gardens are truly one of God's gifts to the gardener. They are a certain gift of mercy to a tired gardener. Here, in creation, God has given us the ground to work and seeds to plant and vegetables to harvest. But he also gives us perennial flowers that return in a sort of cued symphony only known to their molecular cells and rhythms. They return, year after year, in a steady growth and pace, usually out-blooming and outclimbing the year prior. There's an old adage about perennials that says: "The first year they sleep, the second year they creep, the third year they leap." This could not be more true as the first year you plant perennials will be the most disappointing year you have. My father continually gifts us with perennials. My garden flowers because of his generosity. The first year we planted our peonies

## 48 ※ Perennial Care for Next Year

that he sent us from Holland, I knew it meant no peonies in hand that year. The second year they grew tall and green, but still weren't ready to produce bulbs. This year, their stems fell heavy with the red, cream, and pink sorbet petals. Sleep, creep, leap.

With the onset of fall, it's the best time to plant perennials in different places around your beds. Sow perennial seeds. Select what you'll plant in the spring. Plant bulbs and map out gardens. Some perennials need extra care—wrapped in burlap or covered with mulch for the winter. Lavender here especially loves a warm blanket of straw for the long and dark months. Some perennials need to be cut back (irises, lilies, columbine, and others depending on where you live)—a final preparation for the long winter nap. This is the time of year when I'll bring my limes and lemons back indoors, the monstera off of the mudroom porch and back into our dining room, the aloe and tradescantia zebrina off of the east-facing porch windowsill and into the living room. If I want to see all of these steady and faithful plants next spring, my care begins now.

I wonder how often we look for the showiness of the annuals, the flowers that burst through the soil in May and bloom as quickly as they can. No doubt, the annuals are a gift and a joy, but they're fleeting. They are reliable for a season, but next year I'll have to start all over again. Lord, give me the faithfulness of these plants that return year after year, predictably the same and still magnificently beautiful. I have learned to slow down for the seasons you've called me to sleep, the seasons I let my growth creep along the edges of where you've placed me, and the seasons when I leap into full bloom.

And help me to remember that in my seasons of being moved, wrapped, covered, pruned, you have a long view that I simply cannot see. When I feel the pangs of ice and cold, and feel your shears against my limbs, you are looking to see me grow again. You are not cruel. You are not careless. You are for me. The beauty of the garden is the glory of the gardener. My growth and leaping, creeping, and sleeping are under your sovereign hand of care.

Lord, give me a perennial heart.

## Cultivate

Perennials are the flowers that return year after year. They require little maintenance, and after time, give your garden a mature and established look that annuals just cannot seem to do. If you haven't already planned a perennial garden, start here. What colors do you want? What differences of height do you want? How often do you want it to bloom—all season? Just the summer? Only the fall? Take a trip to your local library and find books on perennials, follow perennial gardeners on Instagram, watch YouTube videos, do whatever you can to learn about this specialized type of gardening. Have patience with the work of perennials.

This is the same work that is happening with us. The Lord sees the end; we only see the bare root plants, the empty spots, and we're left wondering if God has any plan for us at all. Give it time. Years even. Our hearts need the work of sleep, creep, and leap too. Trust the gardener that he knows where you need to be.

## 49

# Goodnight Garden

*And on the seventh day God finished his work that he had done,
and he rested on the seventh day from all his work that he had done.*

*F**ather in heaven,* thank you for inviting us into the work of
 your creation.
We have been witnesses to all of it, and we have met you in the
 cool of the day
where you have watered us with your word and listened to
 our prayers that poured into the ground next to seeds and
 seedlings and buried hopes.
You have seen my every movement and moment.
Even the darkest of my nights this year were as light at noonday
 to you, Lord.
There is no detail that you missed.
You who filled the earth and sky by the power of your voice,
you who established the heavens, setting their boundaries in
 place,

you who called forth the green and the flora,
the cicadas and the bees.
It's you who hovered over the face of the deep
who also called forth the vines as they curled up and danced
   toward you.
The earth began to fill with the sound of worship
as all creation praised your name.

> For the beauty of the earth
> For the glory of the skies
> For the love which from our birth
> Over and around us lies
> Lord of all to thee we raise
> This our hymn of grateful praise[21]

There was not a moment of this year that you did not see.
You have not forgotten me.
Through every season and storm,
   early morning sunrise and late autumn wind,
you stayed faithful to your promise.
You called my name in the morning and gave me sleep at night.
And you held me in the expanse of your love.
Lord, another year has passed and I am held once again
by your mercy.
Everywhere I look, I see the gifts of your grace.

> For the wonder of each hour,
> Of the day and of the night,

## 49 ※ Goodnight Garden

> Hill and vale, and tree and flower,
> Sun and moon, and stars of light.
> Lord of all to thee we raise
> This our hymn of grateful praise

And now as the garden closes, remind me of the work that is still to be done —
to love the ones who fill my home,
to labor in your fields with joy,
to harvest the fruit, savor the feast, fill the glasses and fill the table with chairs for all the ones who need the kindness of your bounty.
Remind me to pour out my blood, sweat, and tears for those whom you have called me to love, the easy ones and the difficult ones.
In the places that sift like loam and the places I'm pulling weeds,
may I be so rooted and grounded in your love that
the winter passes without a cold chill in my heart.

> For the joy of human love,
> Brother, sister, parent, child,
> Friends on earth and friends above,
> For all gentle thoughts and mild.
> Lord of all to thee we raise
> This our hymn of grateful praise

Lord, you have shown me that I cannot do this work alone.
Help me to love your church as my own.

Keep me from cynicism, bitterness, fear,
bind my heart to those who I sing with each week,
proclaiming your goodness until the day of your coming.
All of your church in one voice, patiently awaiting the redemption of creation,
including these mortal bodies, tired and weary and longing for home.

> For the church, that evermore
> Lifteth holy hands above,
> Offering up on every shore
> Her pure sacrifice of love.
> Lord of all to thee we raise
> This our hymn of grateful praise

You have given me yourself and invited me to know you.
In all my work and toil, help me to not miss you.
Keep me from working for work's sake.
Keep me from worrying,
the kind that fools me into thinking I can predict, plan, and outthink you.
Oh that my ears could hear the way you shout from and over and to creation
*Mine, mine, mine, it's all mine!* [22]
and soften my stony heart to lift my tired hands,
falling on my weak knees to sing to you,
*Yours, Yours, Yours, it's all Yours!*

For yourself, best gift divine,
to the world so freely given,
agent of God's grand design:
peace on earth and joy in heaven.
Lord of all to thee we raise
This our hymn of grateful praise

## Cultivate

Listen to a recorded version of "For the Beauty of the Earth." Or, if you're so inclined, find a piano or guitar and sing it yourself. Remember the beauty of what God has taught you this year through the work of the garden. Worship him for the good and for the suffering, for the harvest and the losses, for the bounty and the pain.

If you could write your own stanza to add to the hymn, what words would you want to end with "Lord of all to thee we raise this our hymn of grateful praise"? Practice writing this, and give thanks.

# Chapter Epigraph Sources

| | |
|---|---|
| Chapter 1 | Folliott S. Pierpoint, "For the Beauty of the Earth" |
| Chapter 2 | "Sleep," in *The Valley of Vision: A Collection of Puritan Prayers and Devotions* |
| Chapter 3 | J. R. R. Tolkien, *The Lord of the Rings, The Return of the King* |
| Chapter 8 | Luke 8:52 |
| Chapter 9 | Ella Wheeler Wilcox, "Solitude" |
| Chapter 10 | C. S. Lewis, *A Grief Observed* |
| Chapter 11 | "Voyage," *The Valley of Vision: A Collection of Puritan Prayers and Devotions* |
| Chapter 13 | W. B. Yeats, *The Land of Heart's Desire* |
| Chapter 14 | Psalm 74:17 |
| Chapter 15 | Charles Dudley Warner, *My Summer in a Garden* |
| Chapter 16 | Rudyard Kipling, *The Glory of the Garden* |

| | |
|---|---|
| Chapter 17 | L. M. Montgomery, *Anne of the Island* |
| Chapter 18 | Charles Dudley Warner, *My Summer in a Garden* |
| Chapter 19 | 1 Peter 5:10 |
| Chapter 22 | Wendell Berry, "Mad Farmer's Liberation Manifesto" |
| Chapter 23 | Hebrews 6:7 |
| Chapter 27 | Irish Proverb |
| Chapter 30 | Matthew 13:30 |
| Chapter 31 | J. Wilbur Chapman, "Jesus! What a Friend for Sinners" |
| Chapter 32 | Hosea 10:12 |
| Chapter 35 | Anonymous |
| Chapter 36 | John Denver, "Home Grown Tomatoes" |
| Chapter 37 | Gerard Manley Hopkins, "Pied Beauty" |
| Chapter 38 | John S. B. Monsell, "Sing to the Lord of the Harvest" |
| Chapter 39 | Richardson Wright, *The Gardener's Bed Book* |
| Chapter 41 | G. K. Chesterton, *What's Wrong with the World* |

*Chapter Epigraph Sources*

| | |
|---|---|
| Chapter 42 | Paul Harvey, from speech, "So God Made a Farmer" |
| Chapter 44 | Richardson Wright, *The Gardener's Bed Book* |
| Chapter 45 | Robert Farrar Capon, *The Supper of the Lamb: A Culinary Reflection* |
| Chapter 46 | Charles Dudley Warner, *My Summer in a Garden* |
| Chapter 47 | Robert Farrar Capon, *The Supper of the Lamb: A Culinary Reflection* |
| Chapter 48 | Claude Monet |
| Chapter 49 | Genesis 2:1 |

# Notes

1. Thomas O. Chisholm, "Great Is Thy Faithfulness," *Church Service Hymns*, 1923.
2. Lin Manuel-Miranda, "The World Was Wide Enough," *Hamilton: An American Musical* (Atlantic Records, 2015).
3. This is the technical horticulture term for this process.
4. Jake Rossen, "Why Do Birds Sing at Dawn?" November 10, 2020, https://www.mentalfloss.com/article/635843/why-birds-sing-at-dawn.
5. Partha P. Mitra, "The Surprising Reason Birds Sing," TED-Ed, https://www.youtube.com/watch?v=r5_ZSnFDPRg.
6. Excerpt from hymn by Maltbie D. Babcock, "This is My Father's World," #43 in Baptist Hymnal, Broadman Press, 1991.
7. https://www.canr.msu.edu/news/wind_is_essential_to_natural_processes.
8. Oliver Tearle, "The Meaning and Origin of 'Good Fences Make Good Neighbours,'" https://interestingliterature.com/2021/10/good-fences-make-good-neighbours-meaning-analysis-origins/
9. This name has been changed to protect her identity.
10. Beatrix Potter, *The Tale of Peter Rabbit* (London: Frederick Warne & Co., 1901).
11. Sarah Laskow, "Wheat's Evil Twin Has Been Intoxicating Humans for Centuries,"https://www.atlasobscura.com/articles/wheats-evil-twin-has-been-intoxicating-humans-for-centuries.
12. Charles Spurgeon, "The Lesson of the Almond Tree, June 10, 1900, https://www.ccel.org/ccel/spurgeon/sermons46.xxiii.html.

13. Fr. Robert Farrar Capon, *The Supper of the Lamb: A Culinary Reflection* (Garden City, NY: Doubleday, 1969).
14. Tony Reinke, *Newton on the Christian Life* (Wheaton, IL: Crossway, 2015), 191.
15. "When to Water Vegetables," https://www.almanac.com/when-water-your-vegetablegarden-watering-chart.
16. Amy Carmichael (1867–1951), missionary to India and writer. Excerpt from her poem "Make Me Thy Fuel," *Mountain Breezes: The Collected Poems of Amy Carmichael*, 1999.
17. Kathy LaLiberte, "Put Fall Leaves to Work," https://www.gardeners.com/how-to/put-fall-leaves-to-work/5402.html.
18. J. R. R. Tolkien, *The Lord of the Rings, The Fellowship of the Ring*, chapter 1.
19. Janmejai K. Srivastava, Eswar Shankar, and Sanjay Gupta, "Chamomile: An Herbal Medicine of the Past with Bright Future," *Molecular medicine reports 3*, no. 6 (2010), 898.
20. Monty Don, "Switch onto bulbs," https://www.dailymail.co.uk/home/gardening/article-10013923/MONTY-DON-Plant-bulbs-spring.html.
21. Folliott S. Pierpoint, "For the Beauty of the Earth," #44 in Baptist Hymnal, Broadman Press, 1991.
22. Abraham Kuyper said in a speech in 1880: "There is not a square inch in the whole domain of human existence over which Christ, who is Lord over all, does not exclaim, 'Mine'!" See "Sphere Sovereignty (1880)," in *Abraham Kuyper: A Centennial Reader*, ed. James D. Bratt (Grand Rapids: Eerdmans, 1998), 488.